COMPLETE NATURAL FOOD FACTS

COMPLETE NATURAL FOOD FACTS

All you need to know about 600 unrefined foods

Sonia Newhouse

Thorsons

An Imprint of HarperCollinsPublishers

Thorsons
An Imprint of GraftonBooks
A Division of HarperCollins*Publishers*
77-85 Fulham Palace Road,
Hammersmith, London W6 8JB

Published by Thorsons 1991
1 3 5 7 9 10 8 6 4 2

A CIP catalogue record for this book
is available from the British Library

ISBN 0 7225 2488 9

Typeset by G&M, Raunds, Northamptonshire
Printed in Great Britain by
HarperCollins Manufacturing, Glasgow

Acknowledgements

I wish to thank the US Department of Agriculture, and others, who have had the foresight not to copyright their compilations of research findings, thereby making vital information on nutrients freely available to all.

I also thank the Food Sciences Departments of the British Government who, through HM Stationery Office, have allowed publication of some of their data; and Rita Greer and Dr Robert Woodward for allowing me to use information from their book *The Good Nutrients Guide*.

This book is dedicated to Susanna, my daughter, whose encouragement and love helped me through the recovery process of my illness; and to Dr Gordon Latto, who pointed me in the right direction.

Contents

How I came to write this book

When I left Radbroke College in England in 1950 I worked as a supervisor organizing school-meal kitchens, and from there I went on to run canteens and restaurants in England and in Germany. In 1965 I opened an international student hostel in London where I had my first introduction to cooking ethnic foods. As there were so many vegetarians among the students, I was prompted to continue my nutritional studies.

Several years later I opened my own hotel, and it was during this period, in 1975, that I recovered from a crippling arthritic condition of the spine which was threatening me with the prospect of increasing doses of painkillers and life in a wheelchair. I effected this recovery by changing my diet and avoiding refined foods and artificial additives.

Shortly after my recovery, my husband broke a leg and was in plaster for six months: unfortunately the plaster was applied over a lesion which subsequently turned septic. By the time this was discovered the lesion was so deep and ulcerated that it took many months to heal. Owing to this infection his immune system could no longer cope with the bacterial invasion, with the result that an irritating skin condition erupted all over his body. Although the lesion healed the skin condition continued without respite.

Having reached a suicidal state owing to the unremitting irritation, he consulted a skin specialist, whose diagnosis was not specific but who said that cortisone was the only answer, and that my husband would have to take it for the rest of his life. The specialist also said that diet had no effect on skin conditions. All my family knew that cortisone merely alleviated symptoms and did not eradicate the cause, but nonetheless, we decided to try the cortisone so that we could all get some sleep, and to give us time to take stock of the situation.

My whole family had been on a strictly vegetarian diet ever since my successful regime for arthritis, and because of my interest in nutrition. However, it was obvious that for my husband there had to be another answer. When he began to recover I suggested that he should go on a diet consisting solely of *raw* vegetables. The cortisone doses were gradually reduced to zero, and his skin became clear. Rice was then added to the diet and other foods were added at five day intervals, until finally it was found that the skin condition had been caused by a sensitivity to gluten. Over the subsequent years this sensitivity diminished.

My daughter, when very young, was unable to tolerate cows' milk, but eventually seemed to 'grow out' of this condition. However she then developed an intermittent swelling of the lymphatic glands; I decided closer attention to my daughter's diet might benefit her as well. Certain items of food were eliminated in turn for a period of a week, then reintroduced in sequence until adverse symptoms appeared. It finally became clear that my daughter's problem was a sensitivity to cow protein.

After this I became very concerned about the general quality of our food, and felt I had to make a practical protest – I did not want my grandchildren to be brought into a world where the food, water and air were becoming increasingly polluted, allowing allergies the chance to thrive as the immune system was being gradually weakened. The response to my many protests to the food industry over the years was always 'We make what we can sell and no one wants your kind of food.'

In 1983, as a further positive protest, I decided to try to prove that thinking people were indeed concerned about what they ate. I opened the first vegetarian factory to produce frozen foods with natural ingredients and containing no artificial additives. This was also the first frozen food company to declare the nutritional contents of the food on the packaging.

This venture generated a huge amount of public and media interest: I was on the 'On the Market' programme, on Breakfast Time television; I was a guest speaker on LBC, was featured in 'Woman's Hour', and was the subject of many articles in national newspapers and magazines. Feeling that finally my protests had been heard, I decided to give up the business in order to spend more time on the many requests for dietary counselling and other allied activities which I began to receive. During my period as a food manufacturer

I allowed my diet to lapse into haphazard eating because of the pressure of work. I then found that I had become allergic to wheat, an allergy which manifested itself as extreme fatigue and dizziness with an often irresistible urge to fall asleep, combined with frequent problems of recall.

Following this, I spent 14 months in California on business, during which time I counselled on dietary problems and was asked to hold a number of 'wheat-free' seminars sponsored by San Diego State University, the emphasis being upon wholefoods, and the avoidance of wheat gluten, milk, sugar, cheese, and eggs. I am now a freelance consultant on wholefood product development for industry, and a dietary counsellor, currently preparing a cookery book to include those recipes used in my American seminars and based on twenty years of wholefood cooking.

Introduction

The importance of the relationship between food and health first became apparent to me when I recovered from a crippling degenerative disease by changing my diet to one made up of unrefined foods. I began to realize that each succeeding generation enters a world more polluted than that of the last, and it is no wonder, therefore, that our immune systems are no longer fully efficient.

We should all be concerned at the way our food is created at this time. There are chemicals being used to create faster food growth for our vegetables, cereals, nuts, meats and so on. The effect of people's actions and lack of respect for the soil, earth and all that grows from it is manifested by the appearance of allergies, which I feel are direct results of mistreatment of food.

We must all do whatever we can to encourage the growing and creation of food which is sympathetic to our earth – to produce foods the way nature intended. More and more scientific evidence is coming forward to support our case. As a positive action let us talk about it whenever we have the chance, so that we all may create greater awareness of the situation, and try to avoid the foods whose nutritional value has been reduced or altered by refining, processing, hydrogenation and the mutations these cause, as well as foods produced by rapid growing methods.

Nutrition involves providing the body with essential substances to activate vital processes and to promote the growth and repair of all animal and vegetable matter. Dr Michael Colgan in his book, *Your Personal Vitamin Profile* says,

The multiple interaction of these essential substances is the basis of their biological function. And the adequacy of that function depends on the substances being supplied to the body in the same mixture and concentrations that occur in raw, unprocessed foods.

Wholegrains, beans, vegetables, and fruits contain their nutrients in the proportions that nature intended, and can therefore be properly metabolized. When these foods have been 'tampered with' by food technologists, the mix of nutrients becomes altered and is no longer in the correct ratio, thus devitalizing the food and making it of less use to the body.

Processed foods are polluted by chemical additives, and they are devitalized by the many processes through which they pass before they reach the market place, such as heating, texturing, condensing, juicing, flaking, irradiation, freezing, canning, and extraction by the use of solvents. The food industry refines food simply to increase their shelf-life and, in some cases, their appeal to the unsuspecting consumer. The food industry's prime concern is the making of profit; it possesses enormous financial resources, but although it funds research into various aspects of nutrition, it confines that research to those areas from which it will derive the maximum commercial benefit. If we refrain from buying refined and devitalized foods the industry will, of course, suffer financial loss.

Nutritional research is a relatively new science, in which fresh discoveries are constantly being made. When any nutritional evidence is published it is wise to check the source of the data to see who funded the research, and it is usually wiser to believe the findings of researchers who have no vested interests.

Most people are concerned that their diet might not be supplying their bodies with the range of nutrients they require, and as a safeguard they spend vast amounts of money on nutritional supplements, both natural and synthetic, believing such supplements to be the only answer. In fact nearly all these nutrients occur naturally in unrefined foods and it is wise to take this into consideration before taking huge doses of supplements.

This book is a guide to the nature and amount of nutrients to be found in over 600 unrefined foods produced under modern conditions. It makes nutritional and calorific comparisons easy, and enables well-balanced meals to be prepared. There are quick reference lists of foods showing which are the richest in the major nutrients; the guide also gives the average daily recommended amounts of nutrients for varying age groups in the United Kingdom and the United States, together with an additional comprehensive list of all nutrients known to be necessary for humans. Nutrients not given in the tables are available as supplements.

However, we all have individual nutritional needs. For this reason, the toxic levels of nutrients are also given to assist in deciding the amount of supplements to take. Armed with this knowledge, and the nutrient tables contained in this book, it is possible to control the nutrient intake, adding nutritional supplements only where required.

Food repairs and rebuilds the body's tissues, and only by eating a varied diet derived from natural sources is the body given the opportunity to utilize a greater selection of nutrients. The greater the range of foods, the greater the chance that the foods will have been grown on different soils, so producing varying elements for the plants to utilize. Perhaps the most important nutrient, and one usually taken for granted, is water; over 60 per cent of the human body consists of it, it is the most abundant nutrient, representing nearly two-thirds of our bodyweight. Moreover nearly all foods contain water, especially fruit and vegetables. Because water is involved in almost every bodily function, a good clean supply in the diet is essential.

These tables have been researched from international scientific data and from producers over several years; they include only foods that are unrefined, in both their raw and in most cases their cooked states. The nutritional values for a few canned products are included either as a comparison or because they are very convenient. The categories of food I have used are vegetables, fruit, fish, meat, dairy, soya, beans/grain and flour, oils, condiments, herbs, nuts, seeds and spices.

Research into the nutritional values of our unrefined foods has not gone far enough, neither are there any published research papers on the residual deposits of toxic matter to be found on or in foods. Up to the present, food analyses have been based on the quantity of nutrients rather than their quality.

Food is more than just the total sum of nutrients. For example, if one takes an apple and separates its collection of chemicals there would be a disorganized mass of nutrients; if these chemicals are then duplicated artificially and combined, they should, theoretically, produce an apple – but they don't. The reason is that there is a missing element – an animating life-force which scientists do not yet understand. When nature mixes those chemical elements the mass produced is recognizable as an apple in shape, colour, texture and taste, showing clearly that there is an inexplicable life-force at work to produce it.

All animals, vegetables and minerals emit a vital force. A Russian called Kirlian has developed a method of photographing this energy, enabling us to see it being emitted. Perhaps in the future this life-force might prove to be just as important to us as the air we breathe, the water we drink and the food we eat.

What we eat today we will carry around with us tomorrow. Our bodies are able to work only with what we put into them, therefore the quality of our foods is of vital importance. We need more research into this factor and into the micronutrients that may be in foods grown by conventional methods as well as those grown from organic sources. More detailed research into the residual amounts of toxic chemicals in our food and water is also needed.

I hope there are many others who feel as strongly about this as I do, and I am prepared to pledge a percentage of the profit derived from the sale of this book to help set up a research organization to provide us with the information we need.

It seems strange that a Greek physician called Hippocrates, who lived around 340 BC and who is considered to be the father of modern medicine, advised his patients to 'Let food be thy medicine,' yet today there are so few people who do.

1. About the tables

Main points
1. Blank spaces in the tables mean that no uniform analyses are available for these categories.
2. 0 indicates that the nutrient has a nil value.
3. All values are given for edible parts of the foods in their raw state unless otherwise specified.
4. Analysis results are taken from an average value of several samples.
5. At the time of analysis it is improbable that all items will have been grown in identical soils, or been subjected to identical growing conditions, or have reacted identically to transportation and storage conditions before reaching the consumer outlet; all these factors will affect the results of analysis. In the light of these factors nutritional tables should be treated as a guide, as there could be a variation of around 10 per cent either way.
6. The only way to have exact analyses of food is to have it analysed immediately before it goes into the mouth, but as we usually do not have access to a laboratory next to our kitchens this is impractical!

While these tables represent the most comprehensive list of nutrients and of unrefined foods to be found in one volume, they also reflect the inadequate range of foods, and the limited range of nutrients, which have been analysed under controlled laboratory conditions.

There is no common method of analysis for all nutrients throughout the world. This causes confusion not only for the public but also for dietitians and nutritionalists; there is no standard work to which one may refer which covers the whole range of unrefined foods available worldwide.

Most of the reference sources from which these tables have been taken are either from the United Kingdom or the United States. While in some cases differing analytical methods have been used, all those mentioned in this book are considered to be within the 10 per cent allowance. Fibre and carbohydrate values have sometimes been omitted in cases where the analytical methodology used gives results which are not compatible with those quoted in the tables.

Carbohydrates are divided into two parts, simple carbohydrates and complex carbohydrates. Both have subdivisions, fibres being part of the complex carbohydrates. In these tables the analysis of fibre is by the Southgate method, a method that has been used for many years in the United Kingdom and which measures both the soluble and insoluble fibre – called dietary fibre – the value for which is deducted from the carbohydrate value and displayed independently.

However, the definition of dietary fibre throughout the world has been much debated, without a standard definition being arrived at. As there is no definition some nutrient tables give dietary fibre and carbohydrate using differing methods of analysis, which adds further to the confusion. Another twist of this complicated tale is that of all the fibres available in complex carbohydrate, differing selections of fibres are selected for display as dietary fibre.

Unless the data available for carbohydrate and fibre are measured by the Southgate method they have been omitted from these tables. However, it is standard practice to use the nutrients of a similar food listed in the tables as a guideline to assess an approximation of all nutrients, until such time as more data becomes available.

In analyses the moisture content of the food is first extracted and displayed as a percentage, then the nutrients are separated for analysis. It does however stand to reason that if water is expressed as a percentage of the whole then the percentage of the nutrients left will also vary; for example on analysing two peas from the same pod the moisture content of the peas will often be found to vary.

2. Tables of the nutritive values of unrefined foods

TABLE 1: Basic food values

INGREDIENTS per 100g = 3.527oz	WATER g	DIETARY FIBRE g	ENERGY VALUES kcal	ENERGY VALUES kj	PROTEIN g	FAT g	CARBO-HYDRATE g	ALPHA-TOCOPHE-ROL mg	CHOLE-STEROL mg	FATTY ACID SATU-RATED g	MONO-UNSATU-RATED g	POLY-UNSATU-RATED g
VEGETABLES												
Alfalfa leaf concentrate*	55.00		155	649	27.60							
Alfalfa sprouts	91.00		30	127	3.00	TR						
Arrowhead	70.60		107	448	5.00	0.30	21.50					
Artichoke, globe, boiled	86.50		44	184	2.30	0.17						
Artichoke, Jerusalem, boiled	80.20		18	78	1.60	TR	3.20					
Artichoke, Jerusalem, raw	78.00		76	126	2.00	TR						
Arvi/colocasia root	73.90		85	356	1.70	0.20	20.50					
Asparagus, boiled	92.04		25	103	2.59	0.31						
Aubergine/eggplant, boiled	92.00		26	109	1.04	TR						
Aubergine/eggplant, raw	93.40	2.50	14	62	0.70	TR	3.10					
Bamboo shoots, canned	86.80		27	113	2.60	0.30	4.20					
Bamboo shoots, raw	95.90	0.65	12	50	1.53	0.22	1.92					
Beans, broad, boiled	83.70		56	235	4.80	0.50						
Beans, broad, raw	81.00		72	301	5.60	0.60						
Beans, French, boiled	95.50	3.20	7	31	0.80	TR	1.10					
Beans, runner, boiled	90.70	3.40	19	83	1.90	0.20	2.70					
Beans, runner, raw	89.00	2.90	26	114	2.30	0.20	3.90					

INGREDIENTS per 100g = 3.527oz	WATER g	DIETARY FIBRE g	ENERGY VALUES kcal	kJ	PROTEIN g	FAT g	CARBO-HYDRATE g	ALPHA-TOCOPHEROL mg	CHOLE-STEROL mg	FATTY ACID SATURATED g	MONO-UNSATURATED g	POLY-UNSATURATED g
Beans, snap, boiled	89.00		36	150	1.60	TR						
Beans, snap, raw	81.90		31		1.90	0.18						
Beansprouts, mung, boiled	93.00		20	84	2.40	TR						
Beansprouts, mung, raw	90.00		29	121	2.80	TR						
Beansprouts, soya, boiled	89.00		38	159	5.30	1.40	3.70					
Beansprouts, soya, raw	86.30		46	192	6.20	1.40	5.30					
Beetroot, boiled	90.90		31	131	1.06	0.05						
Beetroot, raw	87.32		44	183	1.48	0.14						
Beetroot tops, boiled	92.15		19	79	1.82	0.06						
Beetroot tops, raw	92.15		19	79	1.82	0.06						
Bok choy, boiled	95.20		14	58	1.40	0.20						
Bok choy, raw	94.30		16	79	1.60	0.20	2.90					
Borage	93.00		89	372	1.80	0.70						
Broccoli, boiled	90.20		29	123	2.97	0.28						
Broccoli florets, raw	90.69		28	116	2.98	0.35						
Brussels sprouts, boiled	91.50	2.90	18	75	2.80	TR	1.70					
Brussels sprouts, raw	88.10	4.20	26	111	4.00	TR	2.70					
Burdock root, boiled	75.64		88	368	2.09	0.14						
Burdock root, raw	80.90		72	301	1.53	0.15						
Cabbage, red	91.55		27	115	1.39	0.26						

INGREDIENTS per 100g = 3.527oz	WATER g	DIETARY FIBRE g	ENERGY VALUES kcal	kj	PROTEIN g	FAT g	CARBO-HYDRATE g	ALPHA-TOCOPHE-ROL mg	CHOLE-STEROL mg	FATTY ACID SATU-RATED g	MONO-UNSATU-RATED g	POLY-UNSATU-RATED g
Cabbage, savoy, boiled	92.00		24	102	1.80	0.09						
Cabbage, savoy, raw	91.00		27	115	2.00	0.10						
Cabbage, spring, boiled	96.60	2.20	7	32	1.10	TR	0.80					
Cabbage, white	90.30	2.70	22	93	1.90	TR	3.80					
Cabbage, winter, boiled	93.00	2.80	15	66	1.70	TR	2.30					
Cabbage, winter, raw	88.30	3.40	22	92	2.80	TR	2.80					
Cardoon, boiled	93.45		22	92	0.76	0.11						
Cardoon, raw	94.00		20	83	0.70	0.10						
Carrot, boiled	91.50	3.10	19	79	0.60	TR	4.30					
Carrot, old, raw	89.90	2.90	23	98	0.70	TR	5.40					
Carrot, young, boiled	91.10	3.00	20	87	0.90	TR	4.50					
Cassava	65.50		135	565	1.00	0.20	31.40					
Cauliflower, boiled	92.50		24	102	1.87	0.17						
Cauliflower florets, raw	92.26		24	100	1.99	0.18						
Celeriac, boiled	90.30		25	106	0.96	0.19						
Celeriac, raw	88.00		39	163	1.50	0.30						
Celery, boiled	84.00		15	60	1.00	0.00						
Celery, raw	93.50		8	36	0.90	TR	1.30					
Chayote	94.30		19	79	0.70	0.10	4.00					
Chervil	80.70		57	238	3.40	0.90						
Chicory	96.20		9	38	0.80	TR	1.50					

INGREDIENTS per 100g = 3.527oz	WATER g	DIETARY FIBRE g	ENERGY VALUE kcal	ENERGY VALUE kJ	PROTEIN g	FAT g	CARBO-HYDRATE g	ALPHA-TOCOPHEROL mg	CHOLESTEROL mg	FATTY ACID SATURATED g	MONO-UNSATURATED g	POLY-UNSATURATED g
Chili, hot	88.00		44	184	2.20	TR	8.00					
Chili, red	65.40		116	485	6.30	1.40	9.80					
Chinese leaves	94.00		13	55	1.30	TR						
Collard greens, boiled	96.00		13	55	1.00	TR						
Corn salad	92.80		21	87	2.60	0.40						
Coriander leaves	92.80		20	83	2.36	0.59						
Courgette/zucchini	92.20		25	105	1.60	0.40	4.50					
Cucumber	96.40		10	42	0.60	0.10	1.80					
Curly endive	94.00		20	84	2.00	TR						
Dandelion leaves, boiled	90.00		33	138	1.90	0.90	6.00					
Dandelion leaves, raw	85.60		45	188	2.70	0.70						
Dock, boiled	93.60		20	83	1.83	0.64						
Dock, raw	93.00		22	92	2.00	0.70						
Endive	93.70	2.20	11	47	1.80	TR	1.00					
Fennel leaves	90.00		28	117	2.80	0.40						
Garlic	67.80		117	490	3.50	0.30	26.70					
Gherkins, pickled	618.00		86	380	6.00		17.00					
Gherkins, raw	95.40	1.10	11	46	1.00		1.80					
Gourd, bitter	90.60	4.00	9	40	1.60		0.80					
Gourd, bottle	95.30		16	67	0.60	0.20	2.80					
Gourd, ridge	94.20	1.90	16	66	0.80		3.30					
Horseradish	74.70	8.30	59	253	4.50	TR	11.00					
Kale, boiled	91.00		30	128	1.50	0.70						
Kale, raw	82.50		53	221	6.00	0.80						

INGREDIENTS per 100g = 3.527oz	WATER g	DIETARY FIBRE g	ENERGY VALUES kcal	ENERGY VALUES kj	PROTEIN g	FAT g	CARBO-HYDRATE g	ALPHA-TOCOPHEROL mg	CHOLESTEROL mg	FATTY ACID SATURATED g	FATTY ACID MONO-UNSATURATED g	FATTY ACID POLY-UNSATURATED g
Kantola	87.70	5.80	19	80	1.90		3.00					
Kohlrabi, boiled	90.00		30	126	1.80	TR						
Leek, boiled	90.80	3.90	24	104	1.80	TR	4.60					
Leek, raw	86.00	3.10	31	128	1.90	TR	6.00					
Lettuce, butterhead	96.00		12	51	1.20	TR						
Lettuce, cos/romaine	94.00		17	75	1.70	TR						
Lettuce, crisphead	96.00		13	55	0.60	TR						
Lettuce, iceberg	95.89		13	54	1.00	0.19						
Lettuce, round	95.90	1.50	12	51	1.00	0.40	1.20					
Mangetout, boiled	89.00		40	167	3.00	TR	6.80					
Mangetout, raw	88.89		42	175	2.80	0.20						
Marrow, boiled	97.80	0.60	7	29	0.40	TR	1.40					
Marrow, raw	93.50	1.80	16	69	0.60	TR	3.70					
Marrow, Parwal	91.90	3.30	14	61	1.60		2.10					
Mooli	93.00		24	100	1.00	0.10	4.30					
Mushroom, boiled	91.00		25	107	1.90	0.60						
Mushroom, raw	91.50	2.50	13	53	1.80	0.60	0.00					
Mushroom, Chinese, dried	12.80		284	1188	10.00	1.80	59.90					
Mushroom, shiitake, boiled	83.48		55	230	1.56	0.22						
Mushroom, shiitake, dried	9.50		296	1239	9.50	0.99						
Mustard and cress	92.50	3.70	10	47	1.60	TR	0.90					
Mustard greens, boiled	94.00		90	376	2.00	TR	2.00					

INGREDIENTS per 100g = 3.527oz	WATER g	DIETARY FIBRE g	ENERGY VALUE kcal	ENERGY VALUE kj	PROTEIN g	FAT g	CARBO-HYDRATE g	ALPHA-TOCOPHE-ROL mg	CHOLE-STEROL mg	FATTY ACID SATU-RATED g	MONO-UNSATU-RATED g	POLY-UNSATU-RATED g
Mustard leaves	89.80		34	142	4.00	0.60	3.20					
Okra	90.00	3.20	17	71	2.00	TR	2.30					
Okra pod, boiled	90.00		29	121	2.00	TR	7.00					
Okra pod, raw	91.90		29	121	2.00	0.30						
Olives, in brine	76.50	4.40	103	422	0.90	11.00	TR					
Onion, boiled	96.60	1.30	13	53	0.60	TR	2.70					
Onion, raw	92.80	1.30	23	99	0.90	TR	5.20					
Onion, shallot	86.60		48	200	1.90	0.30	9.60					
Onion, spring	86.80	3.10	35	151	0.90	TR	8.50					
Onion, Welsh	90.50		34	142	1.90	0.40						
Parsnip, boiled	83.20	2.50	56	233	1.30	TR	13.50					
Parsnip, raw	82.50	4.00	49	213	1.70	TR	11.30					
Peas, boiled	80.00	5.20	52	223	5.00	0.40	7.70					
Peas, frozen, boiled	80.70	12.00	41	175	5.40	0.40	4.30					
Peas, raw	78.50	5.20	67	283	5.80	0.40	10.60					
Pepper, green, boiled	93.70	0.90	14	59	0.90	0.40	1.80					
Pepper, green, raw	93.50	0.90	15	65	0.90	0.40	2.20					
Potato, baked in skin	57.00	2.00	85	361	2.10	0.10	20.30					
Potato, chipped	47.00		253	1065	3.80	10.90	37.30					
Potato, new, boiled	78.80	2.00	76	324	1.60	0.10	18.30					
Potato, old, boiled	80.50	1.00	80	343	1.40	0.10	19.70					
Pumpkin, boiled	94.00		20	85	0.80	TR						
Pumpkin leaves, boiled	92.51		21	85	2.70	0.22						

INGREDIENTS per 100g = 3.527oz	WATER g	DIETARY FIBRE g	ENERGY VALUES kcal	kj	PROTEIN g	FAT g	CARBOHYDRATE g	ALPHA-TOCOPHEROL mg	CHOLESTEROL mg	FATTY ACID SATURATED g	MONO-UNSATURATED g	POLY-UNSATURATED g
Purslane, boiled	93.52		18	75	1.49	0.19						
Purslane, raw	93.92		16	66	1.30	0.10						
Radish	93.30	1.00	15	62	1.00	TR	2.80					
Rutabaga, boiled	90.20		35	146	0.90	0.10						
Rutabaga, raw	89.66		36	150	1.20	0.20						
Salsify, boiled	81.20		18	77	1.90	TR	2.80					
Salsify, raw	77.00		82	343	3.30	0.20						
Sauerkraut, canned	93.00		19	79	0.80	TR	4.00					
Sea kale, boiled	95.60	1.20	8	33	1.40	TR	0.60					
Seaweed, arame, dried	19.30		235	983	6.00	0.10	60.60					
Seaweed, hijiki, dried	16.80		173	724	4.50	0.80	42.80					
Seaweed, kelp/kombu, dried	15.80		219	916	5.60	1.00	54.20					
Seaweed, kelp/kombu, raw	73.40		71	297	2.70	0.20	17.00					
Seaweed, kelp/kombu, soaked	87.90		36	150	0.90	0.40	8.40					
Seaweed, nori/laver, dried	11.80		235	983	22.20	1.10	44.30					
Seaweed, nori/laver, soaked	90.10		29	121	2.60	0.80	4.20					
Seaweed, spirulina, dried	5.00		285	193	57.00	7.00	25.00					
Seaweed, wakame, dried	79.99		45	188	3.03	0.64						

INGREDIENTS per 100g = 3.527oz	WATER g	DIETARY FIBRE g	ENERGY VALUE kcal	ENERGY VALUE kJ	PROTEIN g	FAT g	CARBOHYDRATE g	ALPHA-TOCOPHEROL mg	CHOLESTEROL mg	FATTY ACID SATURATED g	MONO-UNSATURATED g	POLY-UNSATURATED g
Seaweed, wakame, raw	79.99		45	188	3.03	0.						
Sorrel, boiled	93.60		19	66	1.60	0.						
Sorrel, raw	90.90		28	117	2.10	0.						
Spinach, boiled	85.10	6.30	30	128	5.10	0.	1.40					
Spinach, raw	90.70		25		3.20	0.						
Spinach, New Zealand, boiled	94.80	0.61	12	50	1.30	0.–	2.20					
Spinach, New Zealand, raw	94.00	0.70	14	58	1.56	0.	2.50					
Spring greens, boiled	93.60	3.80	10	43	1.70	TF	0.90					
Squash, spaghetti, boiled	92.30		29	121	0.66	0.						
Squash, spaghetti, raw	91.60		33	138	0.64	0.						
Squash, summer, boiled	94.00		19	79	1.00	0.	4.00					
Squash, winter, boiled	89.00		39	163	1.00	0.	9.00					
Succotash, boiled	68.37		115	481	5.07	0.						
Succotash, raw	73.10		99	414	5.03	1.						
Swede, boiled	91.60	2.80	18	76	0.90	TF	3.80					
Sweet potato, baked in skin	73.00		100	421	1.70	TF						
Sweet potato, raw	70.00	2.50	91	387	1.20	0.	21.50					
Sweetcorn, baby, canned	92.50		21	88	2.90	0.–	2.40					

INGREDIENTS per 100g = 3.527oz	WATER g	DIETARY FIBRE g	ENERGY VALUES kcal	kj	PROTEIN g	FAT g	CARBO-HYDRATE g	ALPHA-TOCOPHE-ROL mg	CHOLE-STEROL mg	FATTY ACID SATU-RATED g	MONO-UNSATU-RATED g	POLY-UNSATU-RATED g
Sweetcorn, cob, boiled	65.20	3.70	123	538	4.10	2.40	23.70					
Sweetcorn kernel, canned	76.30		82	343	2.10	0.60						
Sweetcorn kernel, raw	76.50		83	347	3.20	1.00						
Swiss chard, boiled	92.65		20	83	1.88	0.08						
Swiss chard, raw	92.66		19	79	1.80	0.20						
Tomato, canned	94.00	0.90	12	51	1.10	TR	2.00					
Tomato, raw	93.40	1.50	14	60	0.90	TR	2.80					
Tomato, green, raw	93.00		24	100	1.20	0.20						
Tomato purée	87.00		16	70	0.64	TR						
Turnip greens, boiled	93.00		21	87	1.30	TR						
Turnip greens, raw	91.07		27	113	1.50	0.30						
Turnip, boiled	94.50	2.20	14	60	0.70	0.30	2.30					
Vine leaves	80.30	5.00	15	64	3.60		0.20					
Water chestnut, canned	86.00		50	209	0.70	TR						
Water chestnut, raw	78.30		79	330	0.20	19.00						
Watercress	91.10	3.30	14	61	2.90	TR	0.70					
Yam, boiled	65.80	3.90	119	508	1.60	0.10	29.80					
Yam, raw	73.00	4.10	131	560	2.00	0.20	32.40					

FRUIT

	WATER g	DIETARY FIBRE g	ENERGY VALUES kcal	kj	PROTEIN g	FAT g	CARBO-HYDRATE g	ALPHA-TOCOPHE-ROL mg	CHOLE-STEROL mg	SATU-RATED g	MONO-UNSATU-RATED g	POLY-UNSATU-RATED g
Acerola	92.30		23		0.30	0.20						
Apple, dried	31.70		243	017	0.93	0.32						

INGREDIENTS per 100g = 3.527oz	WATER g	DIETARY FIBRE g	ENERGY VALUES kcal	ENERGY VALUES kj	PROTEIN g	FAT g	CARBO-HYDRATE g	ALPHA-TOCOPHE-ROL mg	CHOLE-STEROL mg	FATTY ACID SATU-RATED g	MONO-UNSATU-RATED g	POLY-UNSATU-RATED g
Apple, cooking, baked in skin	68.00	2.00	31	133	0.30	TR	8.00					
Apple, eating, peeled	84.30	2.00	46	196	0.30	TR	11.90					
Apple butter	51.60		186		0.40	0.80						
Apple juice, concentrate			275	1177								
Apricot, canned in water	89.10		37		0.70	0.03	5.70					
Apricot, boiled	87.90	1.70	23	98	0.40	TR						
Apricot, dried	14.70	24.00	182	776	4.80	TR	43.40					
Apricot, dried, boiled	68.40	8.90	66	288	1.80	TR	16.10					
Apricot, raw	86.60	2.10	28	117	0.60	TR	6.70					
Avocado	68.70	2.00	223	922	4.20	22.20	1.80					
Banana, dried	3.00		346	1448	3.89	1.80						
Banana, raw	70.70	3.40	79	337	1.10	0.30	19.20					
Banana flakes, dehydrated	3.00		340		4.40	0.80						
Bilberry	84.90		56	240	0.60	TR	14.30					
Blackberry, boiled	84.60	6.30	25	107	1.10	TR	5.50					
Blackberry, raw	82.00	7.30	29	125	1.30	TR	6.40					
Breadfruit	70.80		103		1.70	0.30						
Cherimoya	73.50		54		0.70	0.20						
Cherry, cooking	79.80	1.70	46	196	0.60	TR	11.60					
Cherry, eating	81.50	1.70	47	201	0.60	TR	11.90					
Coconut, creamed	53.80		330	1381	4.30	34.70	6.00					

INGREDIENTS per 100g = 3.527oz	WATER g	DIETARY FIBRE g	ENERGY VALUES kcal	kj	PROTEIN g	FAT g	CARBOHYDRATE g	ALPHA-TOCOPHEROL mg	CHOLESTEROL mg	FATTY ACID SATURATED g	MONO-UNSATURATED g	POLY-UNSATURATED g
Coconut, desiccated	3.00		660	2762	6.88	64.50						
Coconut flesh	45.00		346	1451	3.50	35.00						
Coconut water/milk	94.20		22		0.30	0.20						
Crabapple	78.90		76	317	0.40	0.30						
Cranberry	87.00	4.20	15	63	0.40	TR	3.50					
Currant, black, boiled	80.70	7.40	24	103	0.80	TR	5.60					
Currant, black, dried	22.00	6.50	243	1039	1.70	TR	63.10					
Currant, black, raw	77.40	8.70	28	121	0.90	TR	6.60					
Currant, red, boiled	85.30	7.00	18	76	0.90	TR	3.80					
Currant, red, raw	82.80	8.20	21	89	1.10	TR	4.40					
Currant, white, boiled	85.70		22	96	1.10	TR	4.80					
Currant, white, raw	83.30	6.80	26	112	1.30	TR	5.60					
Damson, boiled, no stone	80.70	3.50	32	136	0.40	TR	8.10					
Date, dried, no stone	14.60	8.70	248	1056	2.00	TR	63.90					
Elderberry	79.80		73	304	0.66	0.50						
Fig, dried	16.80	18.50	213	908	3.60	TR	52.90					
Fig, dried, stewed	72.00	3.10	118	504	2.00	TR	29.40					
Fig, raw	98.00	2.50	41	174	1.30	TR	9.50					
Gooseberry, ripe, raw	83.70	3.50	37	157	0.60	TR	9.20					
Gooseberry, stewed	91.40	2.70	14	62	0.90	TR	2.90					
Granadilla	75.10		45		1.10	0.28						
Grapefruit, flesh	90.89		32	134	0.60	0.10						
Grapefruit, pink, Florida	91.56		30	124	0.55	0.10						

INGREDIENTS per 100g = 3.527oz	WATER g	DIETARY FIBRE g	ENERGY VALUES kcal	ENERGY VALUES kj	PROTEIN g	FAT g	CARBO-HYDRATE g	ALPHA-TOCOPHEROL mg	CHOLE-STEROL mg	FATTY ACID SATURATED g	FATTY ACID MONO-UNSATURATED g	FATTY ACID POLY-UNSATURATED g
Grape, black, flesh	80.70	0.40	61	258	0.60	TR	15.50					
Grape, black, whole	65.20	0.30	51	217	0.50	TR	13.00					
Grape, white, flesh	79.30	0.90	63	268	0.60	TR	16.10					
Grape, white, whole	75.50	0.90	60	255	0.60	TR	15.30					
Greengage, raw, no stone	78.20	2.60	47	202	0.80	TR	11.80					
Guava, flesh	86.10		51	211	0.80	0.60						
Jujube	70.20		105		1.20	0.20						
Kiwifruit, peeled	83.00		61	254	0.99	0.44						
Kumquat	81.07		63	264	0.90	0.10						
Lemon, whole	85.20	5.20	15	65	0.80	TR	3.20					
Lemon juice, fresh	91.30	0.00	7	31	0.30	TR	1.60					
Lime, whole	88.26		30	126	0.70	0.20						
Lime juice, fresh	90.20		27	111	0.40	0.10						
Loganberry, stewed	86.10	5.70	16	67	1.00	TR	3.10					
Loganberry, whole	85.00	6.20	17	73	1.10	TR	3.40					
Loquat	86.73		47	196	0.43	0.20						
Lychee	82.00	0.50	64	271	0.90	TR	16.00					
Mango	81.70		65	273	0.51	0.27	5.30					
Melon, cantaloupe	93.60	1.00	24	102	1.00	TR						
Melon, honeydew, flesh	94.20	0.90	21	90	0.60	TR	5.00					
Melon, water, flesh	94.00		21	92	0.40	TR	5.30					
Mulberry	87.68		43	182	1.44	0.39						
Nectarine	86.28		49	207	0.94	0.46						

INGREDIENTS per 100g = 3.527oz	WATER g	DIETARY FIBRE g	ENERGY VALUES kcal	kj	PROTEIN g	FAT g	CARBO-HYDRATE g	ALPHA-TOCOPHE-ROL mg	CHOLE-STEROL mg	FATTY ACID SATU-RATED g	MONO-UNSATU-RATED g	POLY-UNSATU-RATED g
Orange, whole	82.30		40	167	1.30	0.30						
Orange juice, fresh	88.40		44	186	0.80	0.27						
Orange, Florida, flesh	87.10		46	191	0.80	0.21						
Ortanique	86.00		49	205	1.00	0.20	11.70					
Papaya, no stone	88.80		39	161	0.61	0.14						
Passionfruit	73.30	15.90	34	147	2.80	TR	6.20					
Peach, dried	31.80		239	1001	3.61	0.76						
Peach, dried, stewed	68.70	5.30	79	336	1.30	TR	19.60					
Peach, flesh and skin	86.20	1.40	37	156	0.60	TR	9.10					
Pear, dried	26.69		262	1098	1.87	0.63						
Pear, raw	83.80		59	247	0.30	0.40						
Pear, stewed	85.50	2.50	30	130	0.20	TR	7.90					
Persimmon	64.40		127	531	0.80	0.40						
Pineapple, flesh	86.50		49	207	0.39	0.43						
Plantain, boiled	63.90	6.40	122	518	1.00	0.10	31.10					
Plantain, raw	67.00	5.80	112	477	1.00	0.20	28.30					
Plum, stewed, no stone	86.30	2.20	22	92	0.50	TR	5.20					
Plum, raw, flesh	84.10	2.10	38	164	0.60	TR	9.60					
Pomegranate, raw	80.97		68	283	0.95	0.30						
Pomegranate juice	85.40	0.00	44	189	0.20	TR	11.60					
Pricklypear	87.55		41	172	0.73	0.51						
Prune, dried, no stone	32.39		239	1000	2.61	0.52						
Prune, stewed	69.70		107	448	1.17	0.23						
Quince	83.80		57	240	0.40	0.10						

INGREDIENTS per 100g = 3.527oz	WATER g	DIETARY FIBRE g	ENERGY VALUES kcal	ENERGY VALUES kj	PROTEIN g	FAT g	CARBO-HYDRATE g	ALPHA-TOCOPHE-ROL mg	CHOLE-STEROL mg	FATTY ACID SATU-RATED g	FATTY ACID MONO-UNSATU-RATED g	FATTY ACID POLY-UNSATU-RATED g
Raisin	21.50	6.80	246	1049	1.10	TF	64.40					
Raspberry, raw	83.20	7.40	25	105	0.90	TF	5.60					
Raspberry, stewed	82.20	7.80	26	110	0.90	TF	5.90					
Rhubarb, stewed	94.60	2.40	6	25	0.60	TF	0.90					
Sapodilla/Naseberry	79.30		76	318	0.40	TF	8.00					
Sapotes	62.43		134	559	2.12	0.60						
Strawberry	88.90	2.20	26	109	0.60	TF	6.20					
Sultana/golden raisin	18.30	7.00	250	1066	1.80	TF	64.70					
Tangerine, peeled	87.60		44	184	0.63	0.19						
FISH												
Abalone, canned	65.10	0.00	145	607	24.80	2.00	5.20					
Anchovy, canned in oil	41.60	0.00	280	1165	25.20	19.90	0.00					
Bloater, grilled/broiled	55.60	0.00	251	1043	23.50	0.00						
Caviar, sturgeon, granular	46.00	0.00	262	1096	29.90	15.00						
Clam, canned	69.90	0.00	112	469	16.00	0.80	8.80					
Clam, meat	82.00	0.00	65	272	11.00	1.00						
Cockles, boiled	79.80	0.00	48	203	11.30	0.30	TR					
Cod, dried, salted, raw	52.40	0.00	130	544	29.00	0.70	0.00					
Cod, fillet, raw	82.10	0.00	76	322	17.40	0.70	0.00					
Cod, steak, frozen	83.90	0.00	68	287	15.60	0.60	0.00					
Cod Roe, hard, raw	70.00	0.00	113	476	24.30	1.70	0.00					
Coley	81.00	0.00	73	308	17.00	0.50	0.00					

INGREDIENTS per 100g = 3.527oz	WATER g	DIETARY FIBRE g	ENERGY VALUES kcal	kj	PROTEIN g	FAT g	CARBO-HYDRATE g	ALPHA-TOCOPHE-ROL mg	CHOLE-STEROL mg	FATTY ACID SATU-RATED g	MONO-UNSATU-RATED g	POLY-UNSATU-RATED g
Crab. boiled	72.50	0.00	127	534	20.10	5.20	0.00					
Crab. canned	79.20	0.00	81	341	18.10	0.90	0.00					
Cuttlefish	81.00	0.00	81	339	16.10	0.90	1.00					
Eel. raw	71.30	0.00	168	700	16.60	11.30	0.00					
Eel. smoked	50.20	0.00	330	1381	18.60	27.80						
Eel. stewed	61.30	0.00	201	839	20.60	13.20	0.00					
Flounder, baked with lemon	73.00	0.00	120	502	16.00	6.00						
Frogs' legs	81.90	0.00	73	305	16.40	0.30	0.00					
Haddock, fillet, steamed	75.10	0.00	98	417	22.80	0.80	0.00					
Haddock, Finnan	72.60	0.00	103	431	23.20	0.40						
Haddock, fresh, raw	81.30	0.00	73	308	16.80	0.60	0.00					
Haddock, smoked, steamed	71.60	0.00	101	429	23.30	0.90	0.00					
Halibut, grilled/broiled	67.00	0.00	164	386	23.00	7.00						
Halibut, raw	78.10	0.00	92	390	17.70	2.40	0.00					
Halibut, steamed	70.90	0.00	131	553	23.80	4.00	0.00					
Herring, grilled/broiled	65.50	0.00	199	328	20.40	13.00	0.00					
Herring, pickled	59.40	0.00	223	933	20.40	15.10						
Herring, raw	63.90	0.00	234	970	16.80	18.50	0.00					
Herring, roe, soft, raw	82.00	0.00	80	337	13.30	3.00	0.00					
Hilsa	53.70	0.00	273	1142	21.80	19.40	2.90					
Kipper, baked	58.70	0.00	205	855	25.50	11.40	0.00					

INGREDIENTS per 100g = 3.527oz	WATER g	DIETARY FIBRE g	ENERGY VALUE kcal	kJ	PROTEIN g	FAT g	CARBO-HYDRATE g	ALPHA-TOCOPHE-ROL mg	CHOLE-STEROL mg	FATTY ACID SATU-RATED g	MONO-UNSATU-RATED g	POLY-UNSATU-RATED g
Ling Cod	80.00	0.00	84	351	17.90	0.80						
Lobster, boiled	72.40	0.00	119	502	22.10	3.40	0.00					
Mackerel, canned	66.00	0.00	183	766	19.30	11.10	0.00					
Mackerel, fried	65.60	0.00	188	784	21.50	11.30	0.00					
Mackerel, raw	64.00	0.00	223	926	19.00	16.30	0.00					
Mackerel, smoked	59.40	0.00	219	916	23.80	13.00	TR					
Mussels, boiled	79.00	0.00	87	366	17.20	2.00	TR					
Ocean Perch, breaded, fried	59.00	0.00	217	908	18.80	12.30						
Octopus	83.90	0.00	68	285	13.60	1.10	0.00					
Oysters, breaded, fried	65.00	0.00	200	837	11.00	11.00						
Oysters, raw	85.70	0.00	51	217	10.80	0.90	TR					
Pilchard, canned in tomato	70.00	0.00	126	531	18.80	5.40	0.70					
Plaice, raw	79.50	0.00	91	336	17.90	2.20	0.00					
Plaice, steamed	78.00	0.00	93	392	18.90	1.90	0.00					
Prawns, boiled	70.00	0.00	107	451	22.60	1.80	0.00					
Prawns, dried	13.70	0.00	362	1515	62.40	3.50	15.60					
Prawns, fresh, raw	79.20	0.00	87	354	17.60	0.90	0.90					
Red Snapper, raw	68.00	0.00	182	757	18.40	12.00	0.00					
Salmon, pink, canned	71.00	0.00	141	590	20.00	5.80						
Salmon, raw	68.00	0.00	182	757	18.40	12.00	0.00					
Salmon, red, baked	67.00	0.00	140	586	21.00	5.00						
Salmon, red, canned	70.40	0.00	155	649	20.30	8.20	0.00					
Salmon, smoked	64.90	0.00	142	598	25.40	4.50	0.00					

INGREDIENTS per 100g = 3.527oz	WATER g	DIETARY FIBRE g	ENERGY VALUES kcal	ENERGY VALUES kj	PROTEIN g	FAT g	CARBO-HYDRATE g	ALPHA-TOCOPHE-ROL mg	CHOLE-STEROL mg	FATTY ACID SATU-RATED g	MONO-UNSATU-RATED g	POLY-UNSATU-RATED g
Salmon, steamed	65.40	0.00	197	323	20.10	13.00	0.00					
Sardine, canned in oil	58.40	0.00	217	906	23.70	13.60	0.00					
Sardine, canned in tomato	65.00	0.00	177	740	17.80	11.60	0.50					
Scallop, steamed	73.10	0.00	105	446	23.20	1.40	TR					
Scampi, fried	39.40	0.00	316	1321	12.20	17.60	28.90					
Shrimps, boiled	62.50	0.00	117	493	23.80	2.40	0.00					
Shrimps, dried	25.50	0.00	245	1337	55.80	2.40	0.00					
Shrimps, fried	55.00	0.00	200	337	16.00	10.00						
Shrimps, frozen	81.20	0.00	73	310	16.50	0.80	0.00					
Skate, fried	50.70	0.00	163	580	14.70	9.90	4.00					
Sole, Lemon, raw	81.20	0.00	81	343	17.10	1.40	0.00					
Sole, Lemon, steamed	77.20	0.00	91	384	20.60	0.90	0.00					
Sprats, dried	49.70	0.00	168	704	25.30	7.40	0.00					
Sprats, fresh, raw	76.80	0.00	100	418	19.60	1.80	0.00					
Sprats, fried	33.70	0.00	441	1826	24.90	37.90	0.00					
Squid, dried	21.80	0.00	328	1372	63.30	4.60	3.90					
Squid, fresh, raw	82.00	0.00	75	314	15.30	0.80	0.00					
Squid, frozen, raw	84.20	0.00	66	278	13.10	1.50	0.70					
Trout, grilled/broiled with butter	63.00	0.00	205	858	24.00	10.00						
Tuna, canned in oil	54.60	0.00	289	1202	22.80	22.00	0.00					
Tuna, canned in water	63.00	0.00	158	661	35.00	1.00						
Tuna, raw		0.00										
Whelks, boiled	77.50	0.00	91	385	18.50	1.90	TR					

INGREDIENTS per 100g = 3.527oz	WATER g	DIETARY FIBRE g	ENERGY VALUES kcal	ENERGY VALUES kj	PROTEIN g	FAT g	CARBO-HYDRATE g	ALPHA-TOCOPHE-ROL mg	CHOLE-STEROL mg	FATTY ACID SATU-RATED g	FATTY ACID MONO-UNSATU-RATED g	FATTY ACID POLY-UNSATU-RATED g
Whitebait, fried	23.50	0.00	525	2174	19.50	47.50	5.30					
Whiting, steamed	76.90	0.00	92	389	20.90	0.90	0.00					
Winkles, boiled	79.10	0.00	74	312	15.30	1.40	TR					
MEAT												
Bacon, back rasher, raw	40.50	0.00	428	1766	14.20	41.20	0.00					
Bacon, Canadian style	62.00	0.00	184	770	23.90	8.50						
Bacon, collar, boiled	49.00	0.00	325	1346	20.40	27.00	0.00					
Bacon, gammon, boiled	53.90	0.00	629	1119	24.70	18.90	0.00					
Bacon, gammon rasher, grilled/broiled	52.10	0.00	228	953	29.50	12.20	0.00					
Bacon, rasher, fried	29.70	0.00	465	1926	24.90	40.50	0.00					
Bacon, rasher, grilled/broiled	36.00	0.00	405	1681	25.30	33.30	0.00					
Bacon, regular	13.00	0.00	578	2419	31.50	47.00						
Bacon, streaky, grilled/broiled	34.60	0.00	422	1749	24.50	36.00	0.00					
Beef, bottom round, cooked	54.00	0.00	258	1084	29.00	15.00	0.00					
Beef, brisket, boiled	48.40	0.00	326	1354	27.60	23.90	0.00					
Beef, canned, corned UK style	58.50	0.00	217	905	26.90	21.00	0.00					

INGREDIENTS per 100g = 3.527oz	WATER g	DIETARY FIBRE g	ENERGY VALUES kcal	ENERGY VALUES kj	PROTEIN g	FAT g	CARBO-HYDRATE g	ALPHA-TOCOPHE-ROL mg	CHOLE-STEROL mg	FATTY ACID SATU-RATED g	MONO-UNSATU-RATED g	POLY-UNSATU-RATED g
Beef, canned, corned US style	59.00	0.00	205	858	25.80	11.70						
Beef, chuck blade pot roast	43.00	0.00	382	1599	25.00	30.00	0.00					
Beef, dried, chipped	48.00	0.00	201	841	33.00	5.50	0.00					
Beef, forerib, lean roast	59.10	0.00	225	941	27.90	12.60	0.00					
Beef, forerib, roast	48.40	0.00	349	1446	22.40	28.80	0.00					
Beef, ground	54.00	0.00	288	1205	23.00	21.00	0.00					
Beef, heart, cooked	61.30	0.00	188	806	31.30	5.70	0.00					
Beef, lean only	62.00	0.00	192	806	27.60	9.10	0.00					
Beef, minced, stewed	59.10	0.00	229	955	23.10	15.20	0.00					
Beef, rump steak, grilled/broiled	59.30	0.00	218	912	27.30	12.10	0.00					
Beef, silverside, boiled	54.50	0.00	192	806	27.60	9.10	0.00					
Beef, sirloin, grilled/broiled	53.00	0.00	282	1180	27.00	17.60						
Beef, sirloin, lean grilled/broiled	59.00	0.00	208	870	30.50	8.30	0.00					
Beef, sirloin, roast	54.30	0.00	284	1182	23.60	21.10	0.00					
Beef, stewed	57.10	0.00	223	932	30.90	11.00	0.00					
Beef, topside, roast	60.20	0.00	214	896	26.60	12.00	0.00					
Chicken, leg quarter	42.40	0.00	92	388	15.40	3.40	0.00					
Chicken, roast	68.40	0.00	148	621	24.80	5.40	0.00					
Chicken, wing	34.20	0.00	74	311	12.40	2.70	0.00					

INGREDIENTS per 100g = 3.527oz	WATER g	DIETARY FIBRE g	ENERGY VALUES kcal	ENERGY VALUES kj	PROTEIN g	FAT g	CARBO-HYDRATE g	ALPHA-TOCOPHE-ROL mg	CHOLE-STEROL mg	FATTY ACID SATU-RATED g	MONO-UNSATU-RATED g	POLY-UNSATU-RATED g
Duck, roast	49.60	0.00	339	1406	19.60	29.00	0.00					
Goose, roast	46.70	0.00	319	1327	29.30	22.40	0.00					
Grouse, roast	32.70	0.00	127	533	22.00	4.30	0.00					
Ham	72.50	0.00	120	502	18.40	5.10	0.00					
Hare, stewed	60.70	0.00	192	804	29.90	8.00	0.00					
Kidney, ox, stewed	64.10	0.00	172	720	25.60	7.70	0.00					
Kidney, pig, stewed	66.30	0.00	153	641	24.40	6.10	0.00					
Kidney, lamb, fried	66.50	0.00	155	651	24.60	6.30	0.00					
Lamb, breast, roast	43.60	0.00	410	1697	19.10	37.10	0.00					
Lamb, chop, grilled/broiled	36.30	0.00	277	1147	18.30	22.60	0.00					
Lamb, cutlets, grilled/broiled	45.10	0.00	370	1534	23.00	30.90	0.00					
Lamb, leg, roast	55.30	0.00	266	1106	26.10	17.90	0.00					
Lamb, rib, roast	47.00	0.00	370	1548	21.00	30.00						
Lamb, scrag end neck, stewed	52.60	0.00	292	1216	25.60	21.10	0.00					
Lamb, shoulder, roast	53.60	0.00	316	1311	19.90	26.30	0.00					
Liver, beef, fried	56.00	0.00	217	908	27.00	8.20						
Liver, calf, fried	52.60	0.00	254	1063	26.90	13.20	7.30					
Liver, chicken, fried	64.20	0.00	194	810	20.70	10.90	3.40					
Liver, lamb, fried	58.40	0.00	232	970	22.90	14.00	3.90					
Liver, ox, stewed	62.60	0.00	198	831	24.80	9.50	3.60					
Liver, pig, stewed	62.10	0.00	189	793	25.60	8.10	3.60					
Oxtail, stewed	53.90	0.00	243	1014	30.50	13.40	0.00					

INGREDIENTS per 100g = 3.527oz	WATER g	DIETARY FIBRE g	ENERGY VALUES kcal	ENERGY VALUES kj	PROTEIN g	FAT g	CARBO-HYDRATE g	ALPHA-TOCOPHEROL mg	CHOLE-STEROL mg	FATTY ACID SATU-RATED g	MONO-UNSATU-RATED g	POLY-UNSATU-RATED g
Partridge, roast	54.50	0.00	212	890	36.70	7.20	0.00					
Pheasant	67.90	0.00	162		23.60	6.80						
Pigeon, roast	25.20	0.00	101	422	12.20	5.80	0.00					
Pork, chop, grilled/broiled	46.30	0.00	332	1380	28.50	24.20	0.00					
Pork, leg, roast	51.90	0.00	286	1190	26.90	19.80	0.00					
Pork, pan fried	45.00	0.00	376	1573	23.50	30.00						
Pork, rib roast	51.00	0.00	317	1326	24.00	23.00						
Pork, shoulder, braised	47.00	0.00	347	1452	27.00	25.80						
Rabbit, stewed	63.90	0.00	179	749	27.30	7.70	0.00					
Sweetbread, lamb, fried	59.90	0.00	230	960	19.40	14.60	5.60					
Tongue, ox, boiled	48.60	0.00	293	1216	19.50	23.90	0.00					
Tongue, sheep, stewed	56.90	0.00	289	1197	18.20	24.00	0.00					
Turkey, gizzard, cooked	62.70	0.00	196		26.80	8.60						
Turkey, meat and skin, roast	65.00	0.00	171	717	28.00	6.50	0.00					
Turkey, white meat only	68.40	0.00	132	558	29.80	1.40	0.00					
Veal, cutlets, fried in breadcrumbs	54.60	0.00	215	904	31.40	8.10	4.40					
Veal, cutlets, grilled/broiled	60.00	0.00	217	908	27.00	10.50						
Veal, fillet, roast	55.10	0.00	230	963	31.60	11.50	0.00					

INGREDIENTS per 100g = 3.527oz	WATER g	DIETARY FIBRE g	ENERGY VALUES kcal	ENERGY VALUES kJ	PROTEIN g	FAT g	CARBO-HYDRATE g	ALPHA-TOCOPHEROL mg	CHOLE-STEROL mg	FATTY ACID SATURATED g	FATTY ACID MONO-UNSATURATED g	FATTY ACID POLY-UNSATURATED g
Veal, jellied	68.80	0.00	125	529	25.00	2.80	0.00					
Veal, rib, roast	55.00	0.00	270	1130	27.00	16.00						
Venison, haunch, roast	56.80	0.00	198	823	35.00	6.40	0.00					
DAIRY												
Butter	15.60	0.00	737	3031	0.50	81.70	TR		230.00	54.00	19.80	2.60
Cheese, Brie	48.60	0.00	319	1323	19.30	26.90	TR		100.00	16.80	7.80	0.80
Cheese, Camembert	50.70	0.00	297	1232	20.90	23.70	TR		75.00	14.80	6.90	0.70
Cheese, Cheddar/hard	36.00	0.00	412	1708	25.50	34.40	0.10		100.00	21.70	9.40	1.40
Cheese, Cheshire	40.60	0.00	379	1571	24.00	31.40	0.10		90.00	19.60	9.10	0.90
Cheese, cottage, plain	79.10	0.00	98	413	13.80	3.90	2.10		13.00	2.40	1.10	0.10
Cheese, cream	45.50	0.00	439	1807	3.10	47.40	TR		95.00	29.70	13.70	1.40
Cheese, Danish blue	45.30	0.00	347	1437	20.10	29.60	TR		75.00	18.50	8.60	0.90
Cheese, Edam	43.80	0.00	333	1382	26.00	25.40	TR		80.00	15.90	7.40	0.70
Cheese, Feta, sheep and goat	56.50	0.00	250	1037	15.60	20.20	1.50		70.00	13.70	4.10	0.60
Cheese, full fat, soft	58.00	0.00	313	1293	8.60	31.00	TR		90.00	19.40	9.00	0.90
Cheese, goats' milk, soft	65.00	0.00	198	823	13.10	15.80	1.00			10.40	3.60	0.50
Cheese, Gouda	40.10	0.00	375	1555	24.00	31.00	TR		100.00	19.40	9.00	0.90
Cheese, Mozzarella	49.80	0.00	289	1204	25.10	21.00	TR		65.00	13.10	6.10	0.60
Cheese, Parmesan	18.40	0.00	452	1880	39.40	32.70	TR		100.00	20.50	9.50	0.90
Cheese, quark	80.40	0.00	74	313	14.60	TR	4.00		1.00	TR	TR	TR
Cheese, ricotta	72.10	0.00	144	599	9.40	11.00	2.00		50.00	6.90	2.70	0.50

INGREDIENTS per 100g = 3.527oz

	WATER g	DIETARY FIBRE g	ENERGY VALUES kcal	kj	PROTEIN g	FAT g	CARBO-HYDRATE g	ALPHA-TOCOPHE-ROL mg	CHOLE-STEROL mg	FATTY ACID SATU-RATED g	MONO-UNSATU-RATED g	POLY-UNSATU-RATED g
Cheese, Rocquefort	41.30	0.00	375	1552	19.70	32.90	TR		90.00	20.70	8.00	1.50
Cheese, Stilton	38.60	0.00	411	1701	22.70	35.50	0.10		105.00	22.20	10.30	1.00
Cheese, vegetarian Cheddar	33.90	0.00	425	759	25.80	35.70	TR		105.00	22.50	9.80	1.50
Cream, clotted	32.20	0.00	586	2413	1.60	63.50	2.30		170.00	39.70	18.40	1.80
Cream, double	47.50	0.00	449	1849	1.70	48.00	2.70		130.00	30.00	13.90	1.40
Cream, single	73.70	0.00	198	817	2.60	19.10	4.10		55.00	11.90	5.50	0.50
Cream, soured	72.50	0.00	205	845	2.90	19.90	3.80		60.00	12.50	5.80	0.60
Cream, whipping	55.40	0.00	373	1539	2.00	39.30	3.10		105.00	24.60	11.40	1.10
Egg, battery	74.90	0.00	147	612	12.70	10.70	TR		380.00	3.10	4.60	1.20
Egg, dried	4.00	0.00	568	2362	48.40	41.60	TR		1500.00	11.90	18.00	4.60
Egg, duck	70.60	0.00	163	680	14.30	11.80	TR		680.00	2.90	4.90	2.00
Egg, free range	75.20	0.00	148	614	12.40	10.90	TR		390.00	2.90	4.90	1.20
Egg, quail	72.40	0.00	151	530	12.90	11.10	TR		900.00	3.10	4.70	1.40
Egg, turkey	72.50	0.00	165	584	13.70	12.20	TR		680.00	3.70	4.70	1.40
Egg, white	88.30	0.00	36	153	9.00	TR	TR		0.00	TR	TR	TR
Egg, yolk	51.00	0.00	339	1402	16.10	30.50	TR		1120.00	8.70	13.20	3.40
Milk, dried, skimmed	3.00	0.00	348	1482	36.10	0.60	52.90		12.00	0.40	0.20	TR
Milk, dried, whole	2.90	0.00	490	2051	26.30	26.30	39.40		120.00	16.50	7.60	0.80
Milk, goats'	88.20	0.00	56	236	2.00	2.60	6.60		10.00	2.30	0.80	0.10
Milk, human, mature	87.10	0.00	69	281	1.30	4.10	7.20		16.00	1.80	1.60	0.50
Milk, semi-skimmed	89.90	0.00	46	195	3.30	1.60	5.00		7.00	1.00	0.50	TR
Milk, sheeps'	83.00	0.00	95	396	5.40	6.00	5.10		11.00	3.80	1.50	0.30
Milk, skimmed, pasteurized	91.90	0.00	33	140	3.30	0.10	5.00		2.00	0.10	TR	TR

INGREDIENTS per 100g = 3.527oz	WATER g	DIETARY FIBRE g	ENERGY VALUES kcal	kj	PROTEIN g	FAT g	CARBO-HYDRATE g	ALPHA-TOCOPHEROL mg	CHOLE-STEROL mg	FATTY ACID SATURATED g	MONO-UNSATURATED g	POLY-UNSATURATED g
Milk, skimmed, sterilized	90.90	0.00	32	138	3.50	0.10	4.80		2.00	0.10	TR	TR
Milk, whole	87.80	0.00	66	275	3.20	3.90	4.80		14.00	2.40	1.10	0.10
Whey, dried	4.50	0.00	349		12.90	1.10						
Whey, fluid	93.10	0.00	26		0.90	0.30						
Yoghurt, goats' plain	88.70	0.00	63	263	3.50	3.80	3.90		11.00	2.50	0.90	0.10

SOYA PRODUCTS

INGREDIENTS per 100g = 3.527oz	WATER g	DIETARY FIBRE g	ENERGY VALUES kcal	kj	PROTEIN g	FAT g	CARBO-HYDRATE g	ALPHA-TOCOPHEROL mg	CHOLE-STEROL mg	FATTY ACID SATURATED g	MONO-UNSATURATED g	POLY-UNSATURATED g
Soya, cheese	47.10		319	1321	18.30	27.30	TR		TR			
Soya, milk	89.70		32	132	2.90	1.90	0.80		0.00	0.30	0.40	1.10
Soya, milk, powder	4.20		429	1795	41.80	20.30						
Soya, Miso	41.45		206	860	11.80	6.07						
Soya, Natto	55.02		212	887	17.72	11.00						
Soya, Tempeh	54.90		199	834	18.95	7.68						
Tofu	85.00	0.30	70	291	7.40	4.20	0.60					

BEANS, GRAIN AND FLOUR

INGREDIENTS per 100g = 3.527oz	WATER g	DIETARY FIBRE g	ENERGY VALUES kcal	kj	PROTEIN g	FAT g	CARBO-HYDRATE g	ALPHA-TOCOPHEROL mg	CHOLE-STEROL mg	FATTY ACID SATURATED g	MONO-UNSATURATED g	POLY-UNSATURATED g
Amaranth	86.90		36	150	3.50	0.50						
Barley, light, pearled	11.10		349		8.20	1.00						
Barley, pot, dry	10.80		348	1456	9.60	1.10						
Beans, black, dry	66.00		131	354	8.00	0.50						
Beans, blackeye, boiled	71.80		108	452	8.10	0.80						
Beans, blackeye, dry	11.50		340	1423	22.70	1.60	56.80					

INGREDIENTS per 100g = 3.527oz	WATER g	DIETARY FIBRE g	ENERGY VALUES kcal	ENERGY VALUES kj	PROTEIN g	FAT g	CARBO-HYDRATE g	ALPHA-TOCOPHE-ROL mg	CHOLE-STEROL mg	FATTY ACID SATU-RATED g	FATTY ACID MONO-UNSATU-RATED g	FATTY ACID POLY-UNSATU-RATED g
Beans, blackeye, frozen, boiled	66.10		130	544	8.90	0.40						
Beans, butter, boiled	70.50	5.10	95	405	7.10	0.30	17.10					
Beans, butter, dry	11.60	21.60	273	1162	19.10	1.10	49.80					
Beans, Great Northern, boiled	38.80		117	485	7.70	0.60						
Beans, Great Northern, dry	69.00		116		7.70	0.50						
Beans, haricot, boiled	69.60	7.40	93	396	6.60	0.50	16.60					
Beans, haricot, dry	11.30	25.40	271	1151	21.40	1.60	45.50					
Beans, lima, boiled	71.10		111	464	7.60	0.50						
Beans, lima, canned	80.80		70		4.00	0.29						
Beans, lima, dry	64.00		136	569	8.40	0.52						
Beans, mung, dry	12.00	22.00	231	981	22.00	1.00	35.60					
Beans, pea/navy, boiled	38.30		117	493	7.70	0.60						
Beans, pea/navy, dry	69.00		118		7.80	0.50						
Beans, pinto, canned	78.80		78	325	4.56	0.32						
Beans, pinto, dry	65.00		147	515	8.00	0.50						
Beans, red kidney, boiled	69.00		118	493	7.80	0.50						
Beans, red kidney, canned	77.36		85	354	5.25	0.34						
Beans, red kidney, dry	11.00	25.00	272	1159	22.10	1.70	45.00					
Beans, soya, boiled	53.00		170	711	10.50	4.70						

INGREDIENTS per 100g = 3.527oz	WATER g	DIETARY FIBRE g	ENERGY VALUES kcal	ENERGY VALUES kj	PROTEIN g	FAT g	CARBO-HYDRATE g	ALPHA-TOCOPHE-ROL mg	CHOLE-STEROL mg	FATTY ACID SATU-RATED g	FATTY ACID MONO-UNSATU-RATED g	FATTY ACID POLY-UNSATU-RATED g
Beans, soya, canned	76.70		103	431	9.00	5.00	28.60					
Beans, soya, raw	10.00	18.50	403	1686	34.10	17.70						
Bran, oat			328	1600	16.25	8.00	59.00					
Bran, wheat	8.30		206	872	14.10	5.50	26.80					
Bread, cracked wheat	35.00		262	1097	9.25	3.50						
Bread, cracked wheat, toasted	26.00		309	1295	9.52	4.76						
Bread, French/Vienna	34.00		279	1170	9.70	3.96						
Bread, pumpernickel	37.00		255	1069	9.20	3.50						
Bread, rye	37.00		262	1097	8.30	3.70						
Bread, rye, toasted	28.00		295	1236	9.09	4.50						
Bread, wholewheat	38.30		215	914	9.20	2.50	41.60					
Bread, wholewheat, toasted	26.00		309	1295	9.50	4.76						
Breadcrumbs	7.00		390	1632	13.00	5.00						
Buckwheat	13.20		364	1522	8.10	1.50	84.90					
Bulgur wheat, dry	5.80		352	1473	11.00	1.70						
Chick pea/garbanzo, boiled	65.80	6.00	144	610	8.00	3.30	22.00					
Chick pea/garbanzo, dried	9.90	15.00	320	1362	20.20	5.70	50.00					
Corn, tortillas	45.00		216	904	6.60	0.30						
Corn/maize meal	12.20		368	1540	9.40	3.30	73.10					
Flour, buckwheat	12.00		346	1448	6.00	1.00						
Flour, buckwheat, dark	13.20		332		11.70	2.50						

INGREDIENTS per 100g = 3.527oz	WATER g	DIETARY FIBRE g	ENERGY VALUES kcal	ENERGY VALUES kj	PROTEIN g	FAT g	CARBO-HYDRATE g	ALPHA-TOCOPHE-ROL mg	CHOLE-STEROL mg	FATTY ACID SATU-RATED g	FATTY ACID MONO-UNSATU-RATED g	FATTY ACID POLY-UNSATU-RATED g
Flour, buckwheat, light	12.20		346		6.40	1.20	75.90					
Flour, carob	3.00		182	761	4.00	TR						
Flour, corn/maize, dry	12.00		364	523	7.90	1.20						
Flour, lima bean	10.70		342		21.40	1.40						
Flour, rye	15.00		335	428	8.20	2.00						
Flour, soya, full fat	7.00	10.70	447	871	36.80	23.50	23.50					
Flour, soya, low fat	7.00	13.30	352	488	45.30	7.20	28.20					
Flour, wheat, wholemeal	14.00	8.60	310	318	12.70	2.20	63.90					
Hominy/corn, grits, dry	12.00		362	515	8.70	0.80						
Lentils, boiled	72.10	3.70	99	420	7.60	0.50	17.00					
Lentils, raw	12.20	11.70	304	293	23.80	1.00	53.20					
Millet, flour	13.30		354	481	5.80	1.70	75.40					
Millet, whole, dry	11.80		327	367	9.90	2.90						
Oatmeal	8.90	6.30	401	698	12.40	8.70	72.80					
Oats, rolled, boiled	86.50		55	230	2.00	1.00						
Oats, rolled, dried	8.30		390	632	14.20	7.40						
Peas, dried	13.30	16.70	286	215	21.60	1.30	50.00					
Peas, dried, boiled	70.30	4.80	103	438	6.90	0.40	19.10					
Peas, split, dried	12.10	11.90	310	318	22.10	1.00	56.60					
Peas, split, dried, boiled	67.30	5.10	118	503	8.30	0.30						
Popcorn, popped	4.00		375	569	3.00	TR	21.90					
Quinoa, dry	12.00	4.70	347	454	13.00	5.30	62.00					
Rice, bran	9.70		276	1155	13.30	15.80						

INGREDIENTS per 100g = 3.527oz	WATER g	DIETARY FIBRE g	ENERGY VALUES kcal	kj	PROTEIN g	FAT g	CARBO-HYDRATE g	ALPHA-TOCOPHEROL mg	CHOLE-STEROL mg	FATTY ACID SATU-RATED g	MONO-UNSATU-RATED g	POLY-UNSATU-RATED g
Rice, brown, boiled	66.00	1.50	141	597	2.60	1.10	32.10					
Rice, brown, raw	13.90	3.80	357	1518	6.70	2.80	81.30					
Rice, wild	8.50		353	1477	14.10	0.70						
Rye, wholegrain	11.00		334	1398	12.10	1.70						
Sago	12.60		355	1515	0.20	0.20	94.00					
Sorghum, grain	332.00		332	1389	11.00	3.30						
Tapioca, dry	12.60		352		0.60	0.20						
Wheat, durum	13.00		332	1389	12.70	2.50						
Wheatgerm	11.70		302	1276	26.70	9.20	44.70					
OILS												
Almond			884	3698				39.20		8.20	69.90	17.40
Apricot kernel			884	3698				4.00		6.30	60.00	29.30
Cocoa butter			884	3698				1.80		59.70	32.90	3.00
Coconut			884	3698				0.40		86.50	5.80	1.80
Cod liver			884	3698				14.30				
Corn			884	3698				35.30		12.70	24.20	58.70
Cottonseed			884	3698						25.90	17.80	51.90
Grapeseed			884	3698						9.60	16.10	69.90
Hazelnut			884	3698						7.40	78.00	10.20
Linseed			884	3698						9.40	20.20	66.00
Olive			884	3698				11.90		13.50	73.70	8.40
Palm			884	3698				19.10		49.30	37.00	9.30
Palm kernel			884	3698						81.40	11.40	1.60
Peanut			884	3698				11.60		16.90	46.20	32.00

INGREDIENTS per 100g = 3.527oz	WATER g	DIETARY FIBRE g	ENERGY VALUES kcal	kj	PROTEIN g	FAT g	CARBO-HYDRATE g	ALPHA-TOCOPHE-ROL mg	CHOLE-STEROL mg	FATTY ACID SATU-RATED g	MONO-UNSATU-RATED g	POLY-UNSATU-RATED g
Poppyseed	12.20		884	3698						13.50	19.70	62.40
Ricebran	6.30		884	3698				32.20		19.70	39.30	35.00
Safflower	87.10		884	3698				34.10		9.10	12.10	74.50
Sesame	93.00		884	3698				1.40		14.20	39.70	41.70
Soyabean			884	3698				11.00		14.40	23.30	57.90
Soyabean lecithin			884	3698						15.30	10.90	45.10
Sunflower			884	3698				44.90		10.30	19.50	65.70
Walnut			884	3698				0.40		9.10	22.80	63.30
Wheatgerm			884	3698				149.40		18.80	15.10	61.70
CONDIMENTS												
Arrowroot	12.20		355	1515	0.40	0.10	94.00					
Baking powder	6.30	3.10	163	693	5.20	TR	37.80					
Barmene	87.10		179	795	39.00	TR	1.80					
Dill pickle	93.00		7	29	TR	TR						
Fructose			375	1569								
Ginger root, fresh	87.00		49		1.40	1.00						
Honey	17.20		303		0.30	0.00						
Honeycomb	20.20		281	1201	0.60	4.60	74.40					
Honey, in jar	23.00		288	1229	0.40	TR	76.40					
Marmite	25.40		179	759	39.70	0.70	1.80					
Molasses, blackstrap	24.00		213									
Mustard, prepared	80.00		100	418	TR	TR						
Salt	0.00		0	0	0.00	0.00						
Tahini	0.00		690	2890	24.00	63.00						

INGREDIENTS
per 100g = 3.527oz

	WATER g	DIETARY FIBRE g	ENERGY VALUES kcal	ENERGY VALUES kj	PROTEIN g	FAT g	CARBO-HYDRATE g	ALPHA-TOCOPHEROL mg	CHOLESTEROL mg	FATTY ACID SATURATED g	FATTY ACID MONO-UNSATURATED g	FATTY ACID POLY-UNSATURATED g
Tamari			92	385	12.20	0.40	10.00					
Vecon		2.50	133	564	27.00	1.10	4.00					
Vinegar, cider apple	93.80		TR		0.80	0.20	0.60					
Vinegar, malt		0.00	4	16	0.40	0.00						
Vinegar, white wine			6	22	0.10	0.00	1.00					
HERBS												
Basil, ground	6.43		251	1051	14.37	3.98						
Bay leaf, powdered	5.44		313	1312	7.60	8.36						
Chervil, dried	7.20		237	990	23.20	3.90						
Chives, fresh	91.30		33		3.00	TR						
Dill weed, fresh	7.30		253	1057	19.96	4.36						
Marjoram, dried	7.64		271	1136	12.66	7.04						
Oregano, dried	7.16		306	1280	11.00	10.25						
Parsley, dried	9.02		276	1156	22.40	4.43						
Parsley, fresh	85.10		43	181	3.60	0.60						
Rosemary, dried	9.30		331	1387	4.90	15.20						
Sage, ground	7.96		315	1317	10.62	12.74						
Savory, ground	9.00		272	1139	6.73	5.91						
Tarragon, ground	7.74		295	1237	22.76	7.24						
Thyme, ground	7.79		276	1156	9.10	7.40						
NUTS												
Almond	4.70		597	2502	18.59	54.00						
Brazil	3.00		660	2762	14.00	67.00						

INGREDIENTS per 100g = 3.527oz	WATER g	DIETARY FIBRE g	ENERGY VALUES kcal	kj	PROTEIN g	FAT g	CARBO-HYDRATE g	ALPHA-TOCOPHE-ROL mg	CHOLE-STEROL mg	FATTY ACID SATU-RATED g	MONO-UNSATU-RATED g	POLY-UNSATU-RATED g
Cashew	1.70		574	2402	15.31	46.20						
Chestnut, dried	8.40		377		6.70	4.10						
Chestnut, raw	52.50		194		2.90	1.50						
Hazel/Filbert	41.10	6.10	380	2570	7.60	36.00	6.80					
Hickory	3.30		673		13.20	68.70						
Macadamia	3.00		691		7.80	71.80						
Peanut	1.80		581		26.10	48.60						
Peanut butter	1.10	7.60	623	2581	22.60	53.70	13.10					
Pecan	5.00		666	2787	7.00	67.00						
Pine/Piñon	6.00		571	2390	10.00	60.00						
Pistachio	1.10		593	2482	19.00	53.00						
Walnut, black	4.00		607	2540	25.00	57.00						
Walnut, English	4.00		642	2687	14.00	64.00						
SEEDS												
Linseed/Linquist Gold	6.00	25.00	470	960	23.00	40.00						
Melon	6.00		581	2431	25.00	45.00	19.00					
Poppy	6.78		533	2231	18.04	44.70						
Pumpkin	7.00		553	2314	25.00	46.00						
Safflower	5.62		517	2164	16.18	38.45						
Sesame	5.00		562	2352	25.00	50.00						
Sunflower	5.00		571	2390	21.00	50.00						
SPICES												
Allspice	8.46		263	1099	6.09	8.69						

INGREDIENTS per 100g = 3.527oz	WATER g	DIETARY FIBRE g	ENERGY VALUES kcal	kj	PROTEIN g	FAT g	CARBO-HYDRATE g	ALPHA-TOCOPHE-ROL mg	CHOLE-STEROL mg	FATTY ACID SATU-RATED g	MONO-UNSATU-RATED g	POLY-UNSATU-RATED g
Aniseed	9.54		337	1412	17.60	15.90	67.80					
Asafoetida	16.00		297	1243	4.00	1.10						
Caraway	9.88		333	1395	19.77	14.59						
Cardamom pod, ground	8.28		311	1303	10.76	6.70						
Celery	6.00		500	2093	TR	50.00						
Chili, powder	7.79		314	1313	12.26	17.76						
Cinnamon	10.00		217	908	TR	TR						
Cloves, ground	6.86		323	1350	5.98	20.06						
Coriander, leaves, dried	7.30		279	1168	21.80	4.80						
Coriander, seed	8.86		298	1245	12.37	17.77						
Cumin, seed	8.60		375	1569	17.80	22.27						
Curry leaves, raw	73.00		88	368	9.70	1.70	7.70					
Curry powder	9.52		325	1360	12.66	13.81						
Dill, seed	7.70		305	1276	15.98	14.53						
Fennel, seed	8.81		345	1443	15.80	14.87						
Fenugreek, seed	8.84		323	1352	23.00	6.41						
Garlic, powder	6.00		357	1494	TR	TR						
Ginger, ground	9.38		347	1452	9.12	5.95	70.79					
Mustard, powder			452	1884	28.90	28.70	20.70					
Mustard, seed	6.86		469	1965	24.94	28.76						
Nutmeg, powder	6.23		525	2196	5.84	36.31						
Onion, powder	5.00		238	996	TR	TR						
Paprika	9.54		289	1209	14.80	13.00						

INGREDIENTS
per 100g = 3.527oz

	WATER g	DIETARY FIBRE g	ENERGY VALUES kcal	ENERGY VALUES kj	PROTEIN g	FAT g	CARBO-HYDRATE g	ALPHA-TOCOPHE-ROL mg	CHOLE-STEROL mg	FATTY ACID SATU-RATED g	FATTY ACID MONO-UNSATU-RATED g	FATTY ACID POLY-UNSATU-RATED g
Pepper, black	11.00		238	996	TR	TR						
Pepper, cayenne	8.05		318	331	12.01	17.27						
Pepper, white	11.40		296	239	10.40	2.12						
Saffron	11.90		310	298	11.43	5.85						
Turmeric	11.40		354	480	7.80	9.90						
Yeast, bakers, dried	5.00		287	203	38.00	1.25						
Yeast, brewers	62.50		312	306	37.50	TR	37.50					
Yeast, brewers debittered	5.00		283		38.80	0.70						
Yeast, torula	6.00		277		38.60	1.00						

TABLE 2: Mineral content

INGREDIENTS per 100g = 3.527oz	CALCIUM mg Ca	CHLORINE mg Cl	COPPER mg Cu	IRON mg Fe	MAG-NESIUM mg Mg	MANGA-NESE mg Mn	PHOSPHO-RUS mg P	POT-ASSIUM mg K	SELE-NIUM mcg Se	SODIUM mg Na	SULPHUR mg S	ZINC mg Zn
VEGETABLES												
Alfalfa leaf concentrate*	839.00		1.00	44.50	173.00	3.00	272.00	321.00				4.10
Alfalfa sprouts	33.00			0.90			69.00	78.00		6.00		
Arrowhead	13.00			2.60				729.00				
Artichoke, globe, boiled	39.00		0.06	1.35	39.00		60.00	263.00		66.00		0.36
Artichoke, Jerusalem, boiled	30.00	58.00	0.12	0.40	11.00		33.00	420.00		3.00	22.00	0.10
Artichoke, Jerusalem, raw	14.00			3.40			78.00	442.00		4.00		
Arvi/colocasia root	27.00			1.40				550.00		9.00		
Asparagus, boiled	24.00			0.66	19.00		61.00	310.00		4.00		0.48
Aubergine/eggplant, boiled	6.25			0.31			22.00	248.00		3.10		
Aubergine/eggplant, raw	10.00		0.08	0.40	10.00		12.00	240.00		3.00	9.00	1.10
Bamboo shoots, canned	13.00		0.19	0.50	88.00							
Bamboo shoots, raw	12.00				3.00		20.00	533.00		4.00		
Beans, broad, boiled	18.00		0.43	1.50	31.00		73.00	193.00		41.00		
Beans, broad, raw	22.00			1.90	38.00		95.00	250.00		50.00		
Beans, French, boiled	39.00	11.00	0.10	0.60	10.00		15.00	100.00		3.00	8.00	0.30
Beans, runner, boiled	22.00	5.00	0.05	0.70	17.00		41.00	150.00		2.70		0.30
Beans, runner, raw	27.00	18.00	0.07	0.80	27.00		47.00	280.00		2.00		0.40

INGREDIENTS per 100g = 3.527 oz	CALCIUM mg Ca	CHLORINE mg Cl	COPPER mg Cu	IRON mg Fe	MAGNESIUM mg Mg	MANGANESE mg Mn	PHOSPHORUS mg P	POTASSIUM mg K	SELENIUM mcg Se	SODIUM mg Na	SULPHUR mg S	ZINC mg Zn
Beans, snap, boiled	46.00			1.28			39.20	299.00		3.20		
Beans, snap, raw	56.00			0.80			43.00	242.00		7.20		
Beansprouts, mung, boiled	12.00							100.00		9.60		
Beansprouts, mung, raw	13.00			0.86			53.00	149.00		5.70		
Beansprouts, soya, boiled	43.00											
Beansprouts, soya, raw	48.00											
Beetroot, boiled	11.00			0.62	37.00		31.00	312.00		49.00		0.25
Beetroot, raw	16.00		0.08	0.91	21.00		48.00	324.00		72.00		0.37
Beetroot tops, boiled	119.00			3.30	72.00		40.00	547.00		201.00		0.38
Beetroot tops, raw	119.00		0.19	3.30	72.00		40.00	547.00		201.00		0.38
Bok choy, boiled	148.00			0.60			33.00	214.00		26.00		
Bok choy, raw	165.00			0.80			44.00	306.00		80.00		
Borage	93.00			3.30	52.00		53.00	470.00				
Broccoli, boiled	114.00		0.06	1.15	60.00		48.00	163.00		11.00		0.15
Broccoli florets, raw	48.00		0.04	0.88	25.00		66.00	325.00		27.00		0.40
Brussels sprouts, boiled	25.00	16.00	0.05	0.50	13.00		51.00	240.00		2.00		0.04
Brussels sprouts, raw	32.00	28.00	0.06	0.70	19.00		65.00	380.00		4.00		0.50
Burdock root, boiled				0.77	39.00		93.00	360.00		4.00	78.00	
Burdock root, raw	41.00			0.80	38.00		51.00	308.00		5.00		
Cabbage, red	51.00		0.09	0.49	15.00		42.00	206.00		11.00		0.21

INGREDIENTS per 100g = 3.527oz	CALCIUM mg Ca	CHLORINE mg Cl	COPPER mg Cu	IRON mg Fe	MAG- NESIUM mg Mg	MANGA- NESE mg Mn	PHOSPHO- RUS mg P	POT- ASSIUM mg K	SELE- NIUM mcg Se	SODIUM mg Na	SULPHUR mg S	ZINC mg Zn
Cabbage, savoy, boiled	30.00			0.38	24.00		33.00	184.00		24.00		
Cabbage, savoy, raw	35.00			0.40	28.00		42.00	230.00		28.00		
Cabbage, spring, boiled	30.00	6.00	0.07	0.50	6.00		32.00	110.00		12.00	27.00	0.20
Cabbage, white	44.00	23.00	0.03	0.40	13.00		36.00	280.00		7.00		0.30
Cabbage, winter, boiled	38.00	13.00	0.03	0.40	8.00		34.00	160.00		4.00		0.20
Cabbage, winter, raw	57.00	13.00	0.06	0.60	17.00		54.00	390.00		7.00		0.40
Cardoon, boiled	72.00			0.73	43.00		23.00	392.00		176.00		
Cardoon, raw	2.00			0.70	42.00		23.00	400.00		170.00		
Carrot, boiled	37.00	31.00	0.08	0.40	6.00		17.00	87.00		50.00	5.00	0.30
Carrot, old, raw	48.00	69.00	0.08	0.60	12.00		21.00	220.00		95.00	7.00	0.40
Carrot, young, boiled	29.00	31.00	0.08	0.40	8.00		30.00	240.00		23.00	5.00	0.30
Cassava	26.00			0.90	4.00			394.00		2.00		
Cauliflower, boiled	27.00		0.09	0.42	11.00		35.00	323.00		6.00		0.24
Cauliflower florets, raw	29.00		0.03	0.59	14.00		46.00	355.00		15.00		0.18
Celeriac, boiled	26.00		0.13	0.43	12.00		66.00	173.00		61.00		
Celeriac, raw	43.00			0.70	20.00		115.00	300.00		100.00		
Celery, boiled	0.00			0.50						0.00		
Celery, raw	52.00	180.00	0.11	0.60	10.00		32.00	280.00		140.00	15.00	0.10
Chayote	17.00			0.40				108.00		2.00		
Chervil												
Chicory	18.00	25.00	0.14	0.70	13.00		21.00	180.00		7.00	13.00	0.20

INGREDIENTS

per 100g = 3.527oz	CALCIUM mg Ca	CHLORINE mg Cl	COPPER mg Cu	IRON mg Fe	MAG-NESIUM mg Mg	MANGA-NESE mg Mn	PHOSPHO-RUS mg P	POT-ASSIUM mg K	SELE-NIUM mcg Se	SODIUM mg Na	SULPHUR mg S	ZINC mg Zn
Chili, hot	17.00			1.00			46.00	340.00		6.00		
Chili, red	86.00		0.10	3.60	19.00			1286.00		23.00		0.30
Chinese leaves	76.00			0.26			29.00	238.00		9.00		
Collard greens, boiled	77.00			0.40			10.00	93.00		19.00		
Corn salad												
Coriander leaves	96.00			1.95	20.00		36.00	542.00		28.00		
Courgette/zucchini	30.00			2.40	6.00			202.00		1.00		
Cucumber	23.00	25.00	0.09	0.30	9.00		24.00	140.00		13.00	11.00	0.10
Curly endive	52.00			0.80			28.00	314.00		22.00		
Dandelion leaves, boiled	140.00			1.80			41.00	232.00		43.00		
Dandelion leaves, raw	187.00			3.10	36.00		76.00	397.00		76.00		
Dock, boiled	38.00			2.08	89.00		52.00	351.00		3.00		
Dock, raw	44.00			2.40	103.00		63.00	390.00		4.00		
Endive	44.00	71.00	0.09	2.80	10.00		67.00	380.00		10.00	26.00	
Fennel leaves	100.00							397.00				
Garlic	18.00			1.50	8.00			373.00		18.00		0.90
Gherkins, pickled	133.00		0.60	4.60	73.00			700.00		4633.00		2.00
Gherkins, raw	25.00		0.16	0.30	15.00			225.00		11.00		0.20
Gourd, bitter	19.00		0.27	1.40	31.00			330.00		1.00		0.40
Gourd, bottle	14.00			0.40	14.00			151.00		3.00		0.70
Gourd, ridge	12.00		0.10	0.30	16.00			130.00		2.00		0.20
Horseradish	120.00	19.00	0.14	2.00	36.00		70.00	580.00		8.00	210.00	
Kale, boiled	72.00			0.90			27.00	221.00		23.00		
Kale, raw	249.00			2.70			93.00	378.00		75.00		

INGREDIENTS
per 100g = 3.527oz

	CALCIUM mg Ca	CHLORINE mg Cl	COPPER mg Cu	IRON mg Fe	MAG-NESIUM mg Mg	MANGA-NESE mg Mn	PHOSPHO-RUS mg P	POT-ASSIUM mg K	SELE-NIUM mcg Se	SODIUM mg Na	SULPHUR mg S	ZINC mg Zn
Kantola	25.00		30.00	1.90	21.00			145.00		375.00		0.60
Kohlrabi, boiled	24.00			0.40			44.00	340.00		21.00		
Leek, boiled	61.00	43.00	0.09	2.00	13.00		28.00	280.00		6.00	49.00	0.10
Leek, raw	63.00	43.00	0.10	1.10	10.00		43.00	310.00		9.00		0.10
Lettuce, butterhead	32.00			0.30			23.00	257.00		5.00		
Lettuce, cos/romaine	67.00			1.40			25.00	264.00		9.00		
Lettuce, crisphead	17.00			0.40			17.00	139.00		7.80		
Lettuce, iceberg	0.50		0.02	0.50	9.00	0.02	20.00	158.00		9.00		0.22
Lettuce, round	23.00	53.00	0.03	0.90	8.00		27.00	240.00		9.00		0.20
Mangetout, boiled	41.00			2.00			55.00	240.00		3.70		
Mangetout, raw	43.00			2.08	24.00		53.00	200.00		4.00		
Marrow, boiled	14.00	14.00	0.03	0.20	7.00		13.00	84.00		1.00	6.00	0.20
Marrow, raw	17.00	30.00	0.03	0.20	12.00		20.00	210.00		1.00		0.20
Marrow, Parwal	26.00		0.12	0.50	20.00			230.00		4.00		0.30
Mooli	27.00		0.15	0.40	15.00			228.00		27.00		0.20
Mushroom, boiled	5.70			1.70			87.00	355.00		1.90		
Mushroom, raw	3.00	85.00	0.64	1.00	13.00		140.00	470.00		9.00	34.00	0.10
Mushroom, Chinese, dried	76.00			11.70				1482.00		38.00		
Mushroom, shiitake, boiled	3.00			0.44	14.00		29.00	117.00		4.00		
Mushroom, shiitake, dried	11.00			112.00	132.00		294.00	1534.00		13.00		
Mustard and cress	66.00	89.00	0.12	1.00	27.00		66.00	340.00		19.00	170.00	
Mustard greens, boiled	74.00			0.70			40.00	202.00		15.00		

INGREDIENTS
per 100g = 3.527oz

INGREDIENTS	CALCIUM mg Ca	CHLORINE mg Cl	COPPER mg Cu	IRON mg Fe	MAGNESIUM mg Mg	MANGANESE mg Mn	PHOSPHORUS mg P	POTASSIUM mg K	SELENIUM mcg Se	SODIUM mg Na	SULPHUR mg S	ZINC mg Zn
Mustard leaves	155.00			1.60								
Okra	70.00	41.00	0.19	1.00	60.00		60.00	190.00		7.00	30.00	
Okra pod, boiled	63.00			0.40			56.00	322.00		4.00		
Okra pod, raw	92.00			0.50			41.00	174.00		2.00		
Olives, in brine	61.00	3750.00	0.23	1.00	22.00		17.00	91.00		2250.00	36.00	0.10
Onion, boiled	24.00	5.00	0.07	0.30	5.00		16.00	78.00		7.00	24.00	0.10
Onion, raw	31.00	20.00	0.08	0.30	8.00		30.00	140.00		10.00	51.00	
Onion, shallot	26.00			0.70				297.00		8.00		
Onion, spring	140.00	36.00	0.13	1.20	11.00		24.00	230.00		13.00	50.00	
Onion, Welsh	18.00						49.00					
Parsnip, boiled	36.00	33.00	0.10	0.50	13.00		32.00	290.00		4.00	15.00	0.10
Parsnip, raw	55.00	41.00	0.10	0.60	22.00		69.00	340.00		17.00	17.00	0.10
Peas, boiled	13.00	8.00	0.15	1.20	21.00		83.00	170.00		TR	44.00	0.50
Peas, frozen, boiled	31.00	12.00	0.19	1.40	23.00		84.00	130.00		2.00		0.70
Peas, raw	15.00	38.00	0.23	1.90	30.00		100.00	340.00		1.00	50.00	0.70
Pepper, green, boiled	9.00	15.00	0.06	0.40	10.00		22.00	170.00		2.00		0.20
Pepper, green, raw	9.00	18.00	0.07	0.40	11.00		25.00	210.00		2.00		0.20
Potato, baked in skin	8.00	76.00	0.15	0.60	24.00		39.00	550.00		6.00	34.00	0.20
Potato, chipped	14.00	140.00	0.27	0.90	43.00		72.00	1020.00		12.00	45.00	0.60
Potato, new, boiled	5.00	46.00	0.15	0.40	20.00		33.00	330.00		41.00	24.00	0.30
Potato, old, boiled	4.00	41.00	0.11	0.30	15.00		29.00	330.00		3.00	22.00	0.20
Pumpkin, boiled	15.00			0.57			30.00	222.00		0.80		
Pumpkin leaves, boiled	43.00			3.20	38.00		79.00	438.00		8.00		

INGREDIENTS per 100g = 3.527oz	CALCIUM mg Ca	CHLORINE mg Cl	COPPER mg Cu	IRON mg Fe	MAGNESIUM mg Mg	MANGANESE mg Mn	PHOSPHORUS mg P	POTASSIUM mg K	SELENIUM mcg Se	SODIUM mg Na	SULPHUR mg S	ZINC mg Zn
Purslane, boiled	78.00			0.77	67.00		37.00	488.00		44.00		
Purslane, raw	65.00			68.00	68.00		44.00	494.00		45.00		
Radish	44.00	19.00	0.13	1.90	11.00		27.00	240.00		59.00	38.00	0.10
Rutabaga, boiled	59.00			0.30			31.00	167.00		4.00		
Rutabaga, raw	47.00		0.04	23.00	23.00		58.00	337.00		20.00	25.00	0.34
Salsify, boiled	60.00	46.00	0.12	1.20	14.00		53.00	180.00		8.00		
Salsify, raw												
Sauerkraut, canned	30.00			1.00			19.00	169.00		661.00		
Sea kale, boiled	48.00	12.00	0.07	0.60	11.00		34.00	50.00		4.00	52.00	
Seaweed, arame, dried	1170.00			12.00			150.00					
Seaweed, hijiki, dried	1400.00			29.00			56.00					
Seaweed, kelp/kombu, dried	955.00			11.20			199.00			2500.00		
Seaweed, kelp/kombu, raw	68.00			4.70			64.00	978.00		267.00		
Seaweed, kelp/kombu, soaked	158.00			6.10			9.00	1200.00		430.00		
Seaweed, nori/laver, dried	434.00			28.30			350.00	3503.00		1294.00		
Seaweed, nori/laver, soaked	359.00			3.20			25.00	289.00		157.00		
Seaweed, spirulina, dried	121.00			28.90			117.00	1385.00		1060.00		
Seaweed, wakame, dried	150.00		0.28	2.18	107.00	1.40	80.00	50.00		872.00		0.38

INGREDIENTS
per 100g = 3.527oz

	CALCIUM mg Ca	CHLORINE mg Cl	COPPER mg Cu	IRON mg Fe	MAGNESIUM mg Mg	MANGANESE mg Mn	PHOSPHORUS mg P	POTASSIUM mg K	SELENIUM mcg Se	SODIUM mg Na	SULPHUR mg S	ZINC mg Zn
Seaweed, wakame, raw	150.00			2.18	107.00	1.40	80.00	50.00		872.00		
Sorrel, boiled	0.90		0.28	0.90			26.00	198.00		3.00		
Sorrel, raw	66.00			1.60			41.00	338.00		5.00		
Spinach, boiled	600.00	56.00	0.26	4.00	59.00		93.00	490.00		120.00	86.00	0.40
Spinach, raw	92.00			3.00			50.00	470.00		92.00		
Spinach, New Zealand, boiled	48.00			0.66	32.00		22.00	102.00		107.00		
Spinach, New Zealand, raw	58.00			0.80	39.00		28.00	130.00		130.00		
Spring greens, boiled	86.00	16.00	0.08	1.30	9.00		31.00	120.00		10.00	29.00	0.40
Squash, spaghetti, boiled	21.00		0.04	0.34	11.00		14.00	117.00		18.00		0.20
Squash, spaghetti, raw	23.00		0.03	0.31	12.00		12.00	108.00		17.00		0.19
Squash, summer, boiled	27.00			0.30			38.00	192.00		1.00		
Squash, winter, boiled	14.00			0.34			20.00	448.00		1.00		
Succotash, boiled	17.00		0.17	1.52	0.18	0.179	117.00	410.00		17.00		0.63
Succotash, raw	18.00		0.18	1.83	48.00	0.68	113.00	369.00		4.00		0.16
Swede, boiled	42.00	9.00	0.04	0.30	7.00		18.00	100.00		14.00	31.00	
Sweet potato, baked in skin	28.00							348.00		9.00		
Sweet potato, raw	22.00	64.00	0.16	0.70	13.00		47.00	320.00		19.00	16.00	
Sweetcorn, baby, canned	8.00			1.20				183.00		1140.00		

INGREDIENTS per 100g = 3.527oz

INGREDIENTS	CALCIUM mg Ca	CHLORINE mg Cl	COPPER mg Cu	IRON mg Fe	MAG-NESIUM mg Mg	MANGA-NESE mg Mn	PHOSPHO-RUS mg P	POT-ASSIUM mg K	SELE-NIUM mcg Se	SODIUM mg Na	SULPHUR mg S	ZINC mg Zn
Sweetcorn, cob, boiled	4.00	11.00	0.16	1.10	46.00		130.00	300.00		1.00		1.20
Sweetcorn kernel, canned	3.00			0.60			56.00	97.00		236.00		
Sweetcorn kernel, raw	3.00			0.60			89.00	165.00		TR		
Swiss chard, boiled	58.00			2.60	86.00		33.00	549.00		179.00		
Swiss chard, raw	51.00			1.80	81.00		46.00	379.00		213.00		
Tomato, canned	9.00	78.00	0.11	0.90	11.00		22.00	270.00		29.00		0.30
Tomato, raw	13.00	51.00	0.10	0.40	11.00		21.00	290.00		3.00	11.00	0.20
Tomato, green, raw	13.00			0.50			27.00	244.00		3.00		
Tomato purée	6.00							168.00		8.00		
Turnip greens, boiled	137.00			0.80	33.00		29.00	202.00		29.00		
Turnip greens, raw	190.00		0.35	1.10		0.466	42.00	296.00		40.00		0.19
Turnip, boiled	55.00	31.00	0.04	0.40	7.00		19.00	160.00		28.00	21.00	
Vine leaves	391.00		1.60	2.30	41.00			45.00		2210.00		0.30
Water chestnut, canned	4.00			0.80			19.00	117.00		7.00		
Water chestnut, raw	4.00			0.60			65.00	500.00		20.00		
Watercress	220.00	160.00	0.14	1.60	17.00		52.00	310.00		60.00	130.00	0.20
Yam, boiled	9.00	40.00	0.15	0.30	14.00		33.00	300.00		17.00		0.40
Yam, raw	10.00		0.16	0.30	40.00		40.00	500.00				0.40
FRUIT												
Acerola	10.00			0.20			9.00	68.00		7.00		
Apple, dried	14.00		0.19	1.40	16.00	0.09	38.00	450.00		87.00		0.20

INGREDIENTS per 100g = 3.527oz	CALCIUM mg Ca	CHLORINE mg Cl	COPPER mg Cu	IRON mg Fe	MAGNESIUM mg Mg	MANGANESE mg Mn	PHOSPHORUS mg P	POTASSIUM mg K	SELENIUM mcg Se	SODIUM mg Na	SULPHUR mg S	ZINC mg Zn
Apple, cooking, baked in skin	3.00	4.00	0.07	0.20	2.00		13.00	100.00		2.00	2.00	0.10
Apple, eating, peeled	4.00	1.00	0.04	0.30	5.00		8.00	120.00		2.00	6.00	0.10
Apple butter	14.00			17.00			36.00	256.00		2.00		
Apple juice, concentrate	450.00		0.45	4.15	355.00			9500.00				
Apricot, canned in water	11.80			0.30			15.80	245.00		0.88		
Apricot, boiled	15.00	TR	0.10	0.30	10.00		18.00	270.00		TR	5.00	0.10
Apricot, dried	92.00	35.00	0.27	4.10	65.00	0.27	120.00	1880.00		56.00	160.00	0.20
Apricot, dried, boiled	34.00	13.00	0.10	1.50	24.00		44.00	700.00		21.00	59.00	0.10
Apricot, raw	17.00	TR	0.12	0.40	12.00		21.00	320.00		TR	6.00	0.10
Avocado	15.00	6.00	0.21	1.50	29.00		31.00	400.00		2.00	19.00	
Banana, dried	22.00		0.39	1.10	108.00	0.57	74.00	1491.00		3.00		0.60
Banana, raw	7.00	79.00	0.16	0.40	42.00	0.15	28.00	350.00		1.00	13.00	0.20
Banana flakes, dehydrated	32.00			2.80			104.00	1477.00		4.00		
Bilberry	10.00	5.00	0.11	0.70	2.00		9.00	65.00		1.00		0.10
Blackberry, boiled	54.00	19.00	0.10	0.80	26.00		21.00	180.00		3.00	8.00	
Blackberry, raw	63.00	22.00	0.12	0.90	30.00		24.00	210.00		4.00	9.00	
Breadfruit	33.00			1.20			32.00	439.00		15.00		
Cherimoya	13.00			0.28			23.00					
Cherry, cooking	20.00	TR	0.10	0.30	12.00	0.10	21.00	310.00		4.00	8.00	0.10
Cherry, eating	16.00	TR	0.07	0.40	10.00	0.09	17.00	280.00		3.00	7.00	0.10
Coconut, creamed	11.00			2.30								

INGREDIENTS per 100g = 3.527oz	CALCIUM mg Ca	CHLORINE mg Cl	COPPER mg Cu	IRON mg Fe	MAG-NESIUM mg Mg	MANGA-NESE mg Mn	PHOSPHO-RUS mg P	POT-ASSIUM mg K	SELE-NIUM mcg Se	SODIUM mg Na	SULPHUR mg S	ZINC mg Zn
Coconut, desiccated	26.00		0.79	3.32	90.00		206.00	543.00		37.00		2.01
Coconut flesh	13.30			22.00			95.50	255.00		22.20		
Coconut water/milk	20.00			0.30			13.00	147.00		255.00		
Crabapple	18.00		0.06	0.36	7.00	0.10	15.00	194.00		1.00		
Cranberry	15.00	TR	0.14	1.10	8.00		11.00	120.00		2.00	11.00	
Currant, black, boiled	51.00	13.00	0.12	1.10	16.00		37.00	320.00		3.00	28.00	
Currant, black, dried	95.00	16.00	0.48	1.80	36.00		40.00	710.00		20.00	31.00	0.10
Currant, black, raw	60.00	15.00	0.14	1.30	17.00		43.00	370.00		3.00	33.00	
Currant, red, boiled	31.00	12.00	10.00	1.00	11.00		26.00	240.00		2.00	25.00	
Currant, red, raw	36.00	14.00	0.12	1.20	13.00		30.00	280.00		2.00	29.00	
Currant, white, boiled	19.00	9.00	0.12	0.80	11.00		24.00	250.00		2.00	21.00	
Currant, white, raw	22.00	11.00	0.14	0.90	13.00	0.18	28.00	290.00		2.00	24.00	
Damson, boiled, no stone	20.00	TR	0.07	0.30	10.00		14.00	240.00		2.00	5.00	0.10
Date, dried, no stone	68.00	290.00	0.21	1.60	59.00		64.00	750.00		5.00	51.00	0.30
Elderberry	38.00			1.60			39.00	280.00				
Fig, dried	280.00	170.00	0.24	4.20	92.00	0.30	92.00	1010.00		87.00	81.00	0.90
Fig, dried, stewed	160.00	94.00	0.13	2.30	51.00	0.16	51.00	560.00		48.00	45.00	0.50
Fig, raw	34.00	18.00	0.06	0.40	20.00	0.12	32.00	270.00		2.00	13.00	0.30
Gooseberry, ripe, raw	19.00	11.00	0.15	0.60	9.00	0.14	19.00	170.00		1.00	14.00	0.10
Gooseberry, stewed	24.00	6.00	0.11	0.30	6.00		29.00	180.00		2.00	14.00	0.10
Granadilla	5.70			0.85			34.00	180.00		14.00		
Grapefruit, flesh	12.00		0.04	0.09	8.00	0.01	8.00	139.00		0.00		0.07
Grapefruit, pink, Florida	15.00		0.04	0.12	8.00	0.01	9.00	127.00		0.00		0.07

INGREDIENTS per 100g = 3.527oz

	CALCIUM mg Ca	CHLORINE mg Cl	COPPER mg Cu	IRON mg Fe	MAGNESIUM mg Mg	MANGANESE mg Mn	PHOSPHORUS mg P	POTASSIUM mg K	SELENIUM mcg Se	SODIUM mg Na	SULPHUR mg S	ZINC mg Zn
Grape, black, flesh	4.00	TR	0.80	0.30	4.00		16.00	320.00		2.00	7.00	0.10
Grape, black, whole	4.00	TR	0.07	0.30	3.00		14.00	270.00		1.00	6.00	0.10
Grape, white, flesh	19.00	TR	0.10	0.30	7.00		22.00	250.00		2.00	9.00	0.10
Grape, white, whole	18.00	TR	0.10	0.30	6.00		21.00	240.00		2.00	9.00	0.10
Greengage, raw, no stone	17.00	1.00	0.08	0.40	8.00	0.14	23.00	310.00		1.00	3.00	0.10
Guava, flesh	20.00		0.10	0.31	10.00		25.00	284.00		3.00		0.23
Jujube	29.00			0.70			37.00	269.00		3.00		
Kiwifruit, peeled	26.00			0.40	30.00		40.00	332.00		5.00		
Kumquat	44.00		0.11	0.39	13.00	0.09	19.00	195.00		6.00		0.08
Lemon, whole	110.00	5.00	0.26	0.40	12.00		21.00	160.00		6.00	12.00	0.10
Lemon juice, fresh	8.00	3.00	0.13	0.10	7.00		10.00	140.00		2.00	2.00	TR
Lime, whole	33.00		0.06	0.60	0.00	0.06	18.00	102.00		2.00		0.11
Lime juice, fresh	9.00		0.03	0.04	0.00	0.00	7.00	108.00		1.00		0.06
Loganberry, stewed	32.00	15.00	0.13	1.30	23.00		22.00	240.00		3.00	17.00	
Loganberry, whole	35.00	16.00	0.14	1.40	25.00		24.00	260.00		3.00	18.00	
Loquat	16.00		0.04	0.28	13.00	0.15	27.00	266.00		1.00		0.05
Lychee	8.00	3.00		0.50	10.00		35.00	170.00		3.00	19.00	
Mango	10.00		0.11	0.13	9.00	0.02	11.00	156.00		2.00		0.04
Melon, cantaloupe	19.00	44.00	0.04	0.80	20.00		30.00	320.00		14.00	12.00	0.10
Melon, honeydew, flesh	14.00	45.00	0.04	0.20	13.00		9.00	220.00		20.00	6.00	0.10
Melon, water, flesh	5.00		0.03	0.30	11.00		8.00	120.00		4.00		0.10
Mulberry	39.00			1.85	18.00		38.00	194.00		10.00		
Nectarine	5.00		0.07	0.15	8.00	0.04	16.00	212.00		0.00		0.09

INGREDIENTS per 100g = 3.527oz	CALCIUM mg Ca	CHLORINE mg Cl	COPPER mg Cu	IRON mg Fe	MAGNESIUM mg Mg	MANGANESE mg Mn	PHOSPHORUS mg P	POTASSIUM mg K	SELENIUM mcg Se	SODIUM mg Na	SULPHUR mg S	ZINC mg Zn
Orange, whole	70.00			0.80	14.00		22.00	196.00		2.00		
Orange juice, fresh	10.00	37.00	0.04	0.17	11.00	0.02	11.00	190.00		1.00		0.04
Orange, Florida, flesh	43.00		0.03	0.09	10.00	0.02	12.00	169.00		0.00		0.08
Ortanique	41.00			0.40								
Papaya, no stone	24.00		0.01	0.10	10.00	0.01	5.00	257.00		3.00		0.07
Passionfruit	16.00		0.12	1.10	39.00		54.00	350.00		28.00	19.00	
Peach, dried	28.00		0.36	4.06	42.00	0.30	119.00	996.00		7.00		0.57
Peach, dried, stewed	13.00	4.00	0.23	2.50	20.00		44.00	410.00		2.00	89.00	0.10
Peach, flesh and skin	5.00	TR	0.05	0.40	8.00		19.00	260.00		3.00	6.00	0.39
Pear, dried	34.00		0.37	2.10	33.00	0.32	59.00	533.00		6.00		0.10
Pear, raw	11.00		0.10	0.25	6.00	0.07	11.00	125.00		0.00		
Pear, stewed	6.00	2.00	0.09	0.20	3.00		13.00	85.00		3.00	3.00	0.10
Persimmon	27.00			2.50			26.00	310.00		1.00		
Pineapple, flesh	7.00		0.11	0.37	14.00	1.60	7.00	113.00		1.00		0.08
Plantain, boiled	9.00	50.00	0.10	0.40	34.00		34.00	330.00		4.00		0.20
Plantain, raw	7.00	80.00	0.16	0.50	33.00		35.00	350.00		1.00	15.00	0.10
Plum, stewed, no stone	12.00	TR	0.08	0.30			12.00	160.00		2.00	3.00	TR
Plum, raw, flesh	11.00	TR	0.10	0.40	6.00		16.00	190.00		2.00	4.00	TR
Pomegranate, raw	3.00			0.30	7.00		8.00	259.00		3.00		
Pomegranate juice	3.00	53.00	0.07	0.20	3.00		8.00	200.00		1.00	4.00	
Pricklypear	56.00			0.30	85.00		24.00	220.00		5.00		
Prune, dried, no stone	51.00		0.43	2.48	45.00	0.22	79.00	745.00		4.00		0.53
Prune, stewed	23.00		0.19	1.11	0.10	0.09	35.00	334.00		2.00		0.24
Quince	11.00		0.13	0.70	8.00		17.00	197.00		4.00		

INGREDIENTS per 100g = 3.527oz

INGREDIENTS	CALCIUM mg Ca	CHLORINE mg Cl	COPPER mg Cu	IRON mg Fe	MAGNESIUM mg Mg	MANGANESE mg Mn	PHOSPHORUS mg P	POTASSIUM mg K	SELENIUM mcg Se	SODIUM mg Na	SULPHUR mg S	ZINC mg Zn
Raisin	61.00	9.00	0.24	1.60	42.00	0.00	33.00	860.00		52.00	23.00	0.10
Raspberry, raw	41.00	22.00	0.21	1.20	22.00		29.00	220.00		3.00	17.00	0.46
Raspberry, stewed	43.00	23.00	0.22	1.30	23.00		31.00	230.00		3.00	18.00	
Rhubarb, stewed	93.00	81.00	0.12	0.40	13.00		19.00	400.00		2.00	7.00	
Sapodilla/Naseberry	27.00			0.60				181.00		3.00		
Sapotes	39.00			1.00	30.00		28.00	344.00		10.00		
Strawberry	22.00	18.00	0.13	0.70	12.00		23.00	160.00		2.00	13.00	0.10
Sultana/golden raisin	52.00	16.00	0.35	1.80	35.00		95.00	860.00		53.00	44.00	0.10
Tangerine, peeled	14.00		0.03	0.10	12.00	0.03	10.00	157.00		1.00		
FISH												
Abalone, canned	10.00			8.80				110.00		990.00		
Anchovy, canned in oil	299.00	1130.00	0.17	4.10		0.03				3930.00		3.20
Bloater, grilled/broiled	120.00			2.20	56.00		360.00	225.00		700.00	310.00	
Caviar, sturgeon, granular	276.00			11.80	45.00		355.00	450.00		2200.00		
Clam, canned	74.00			8.00				180.00		1200.00		
Clam, meat	59.00			2.60			138.00	154.00		102.00		
Cockles, boiled	130.00		0.28	26.00	51.00		200.00	43.00		3520.00	320.00	1.20
Cod, dried, salted, raw	225.00	5220.00										
Cod, fillet, raw	16.00	110.00	0.06	0.30	23.00		170.00	320.00		77.00	200.00	0.40
Cod, steak, frozen	11.00	95.00	0.06	0.30	22.00		160.00	310.00		68.00	180.00	0.30
Cod Roe, hard, raw												
Coley	14.00	200.00		0.50	23.00		190.00	260.00		73.00	190.00	

INGREDIENTS per 100g = 3.527oz	CALCIUM mg Ca	CHLORINE mg Cl	COPPER mg Cu	IRON mg Fe	MAGNESIUM mg Mg	MANGANESE mg Mn	PHOSPHORUS mg P	POTASSIUM mg K	SELENIUM mcg Se	SODIUM mg Na	SULPHUR mg S	ZINC mg Zn
Crab, boiled	29.00	570.00	4.80	1.30	48.00		350.00	270.00		370.00	470.00	5.50
Crab, canned	120.00	830.00	0.42	2.80	32.00		140.00	100.00		550.00		5.00
Cuttlefish	27.00			0.80				273.00				
Eel, raw	19.00	57.00	0.05	0.70	19.00		220.00	270.00		89.00	190.00	0.50
Eel, smoked												
Eel, stewed	21.00	53.00	0.06	0.90	20.00		230.00	250.00		84.00	230.00	0.60
Flounder, baked with lemon	13.00			0.30			187.00			145.00		
Frogs' legs	18.00			1.50			147.00					
Haddock, fillet, steamed	55.00	140.00	0.13	0.70	28.00		230.00	320.00		120.00	300.00	0.40
Haddock, Finnan												
Haddock, fresh, raw	18.00	160.00	0.19	0.60	23.00		170.00	300.00		120.00	220.00	0.30
Haddock, smoked, steamed	58.00	1900.00		1.00	25.00		250.00	290.00		1220.00	250.00	
Halibut, grilled/broiled	16.00			0.80			242.00	518.00		121.00		
Halibut, raw	10.00	60.00	0.05	0.50	17.00		190.00	260.00		84.00	190.00	
Halibut, steamed	13.00	80.00	0.07	0.60	23.00		260.00	340.00		110.00	260.00	
Herring, grilled/broiled	33.00	220.00	0.11	1.00	32.00		240.00	370.00		170.00	230.00	0.50
Herring, pickled	34.00			1.00			150.00	100.00		1000.00		
Herring, raw	33.00	76.00	0.12	0.80	29.00		210.00	340.00		67.00	190.00	0.50
Herring, roe, soft, raw												
Hilsa	180.00			2.10								
Kipper, baked	65.00	1520.00		1.40	48.00		430.00	520.00		990.00	280.00	

INGREDIENTS
per 100g = 3.527oz

INGREDIENTS	CALCIUM mg Ca	CHLORINE mg Cl	COPPER mg Cu	IRON mg Fe	MAGNESIUM mg Mg	MANGANESE mg Mn	PHOSPHORUS mg P	POTASSIUM mg K	SELENIUM mcg Se	SODIUM mg Na	SULPHUR mg S	ZINC mg Zn
Ling Cod	62.00			0.80	34.00		280.00	433.00		59.00		
Lobster, boiled	185.00	530.00	1.70	2.10			274.00	260.00		330.00	510.00	1.80
Mackerel, canned	28.00	110.00	0.20	1.20	35.00		280.00	420.00		150.00	210.00	
Mackerel, fried	24.00	97.00	0.19	1.00	30.00		240.00	360.00		130.00	180.00	
Mackerel, raw												0.50
Mackerel, smoked												
Mussels, boiled	200.00	320.00	0.48	7.70	25.00		330.00	92.00		210.00	350.00	2.10
Ocean Perch, breaded, fried	36.00			1.40			224.00	283.00		162.00		
Octopus	12.00			0.90								
Oysters, breaded, fried	108.00			6.60			162.00	142.00		155.00		
Oysters, raw	190.00	820.00	7.60	6.00	42.00		270.00	260.00		510.00	250.00	45.00
Pilchard, canned in tomato	300.00											
Plaice, raw	51.00	580.00	0.19	2.70	39.00		350.00	420.00		370.00	240.00	1.60
Plaice, steamed	38.00	170.00	0.05	0.30	22.00		180.00	280.00		120.00	250.00	0.50
Prawns, boiled	150.00	110.00	0.70	1.10	24.00		250.00	280.00		120.00	370.00	1.60
Prawns, dried	236.00	2550.00		4.60	42.00		350.00	260.00		1590.00		
Prawns, fresh, raw	79.00			1.60				333.00		185.00		
Red Snapper, raw	34.00			1.00				373.00		120.00		
Salmon, pink, canned	196.00			0.80			285.00	361.00		509.00		
Salmon, raw	27.00	59.00	0.20	0.70	26.00		280.00	310.00		98.00	170.00	0.80
Salmon, red, baked	26.00			0.50			269.00	305.00		55.00		
Salmon, red, canned	93.00	880.00	0.09	1.40	30.00		240.00	300.00		570.00	220.00	0.90
Salmon, smoked	19.00	2850.00	0.09	0.60	32.00		250.00	420.00		1880.00		0.40

INGREDIENTS per 100g = 3.527oz

	CALCIUM mg Ca	CHLORINE mg Cl	COPPER mg Cu	IRON mg Fe	MAGNESIUM mg Mg	MANGANESE mg Mn	PHOSPHORUS mg P	POTASSIUM mg K	SELENIUM mcg Se	SODIUM mg Na	SULPHUR mg S	ZINC mg Zn
Salmon, steamed	29.00	64.00		0.80	29.00		300.00	330.00		110.00	190.00	
Sardine, canned in oil	550.00	1000.00	0.19	2.90	52.00		520.00	430.00		650.00	310.00	3.00
Sardine, canned in tomato	460.00	1110.00	0.23	4.60	51.00		400.00	410.00		700.00	230.00	2.70
Scallop, steamed	120.00	410.00		3.00	38.00		340.00	480.00		270.00	570.00	
Scampi, fried	99.00	740.00	0.22	1.10	30.00		310.00	390.00		380.00		0.60
Shrimps, boiled	320.00	5850.00	0.80	1.80	110.00		270.00	400.00		3840.00	340.00	5.30
Shrimps, dried	1200.00		0.96	21.30	291.00			495.00		4325.00		3.70
Shrimps, fried	61.00			2.00			154.00	189.00		384.00		
Shrimps, frozen	128.00			2.60	47.00			75.00		375.00		
Skate, fried	40.00	140.00	0.15	0.80	22.00		150.00	200.00		110.00	210.00	1.10
Sole, Lemon, raw	17.00	97.00	0.07	0.50	17.00		200.00	230.00		95.00	200.00	0.70
Sole, Lemon, steamed	21.00	120.00	0.10	0.60	20.00		250.00	280.00		120.00	240.00	
Sprats, dried	201.00		0.12	1.90	73.00			150.00		5210.00		1.90
Sprats, fresh, raw	39.00		4.10	3.20				512.00		190.00		
Sprats, fried	710.00	180.00		4.50	46.00		640.00	410.00		130.00	280.00	
Squid, dried	55.00			4.00				604.00		944.00		
Squid, fresh, raw	15.00			1.00				266.00		176.00		
Squid, frozen, raw	13.00		0.68	0.20	36.00			145.00		185.00		1.20
Trout, grilled/broiled with butter	30.00			1.00			304.00	349.00		143.00		
Tuna, canned in oil	7.00	690.00	0.09	1.10	28.00		190.00	280.00		420.00		0.80
Tuna, canned in water	20.00			0.70			237.00	300.00		550.00		
Tuna, raw												
Whelks, boiled	54.00	590.00	7.20	6.20	160.00		230.00	320.00		270.00	450.00	7.20

INGREDIENTS per 100g = 3.527oz	CALCIUM mg Ca	CHLORINE mg Cl	COPPER mg Cu	IRON mg Fe	MAG-NESIUM mg Mg	MANGA-NESE mg Mn	PHOSPHO-RUS mg P	POT-ASSIUM mg K	SELE-NIUM mcg Se	SODIUM mg Na	SULPHUR mg S	ZINC mg Zn
Whitebait, fried	860.00	330.00		5.10	50.00		860.00	110.00		230.00	270.00	
Whiting, steamed	42.00	93.00		1.00	28.00		190.00	300.00		130.00	310.00	
Winkles, boiled	140.00	1800.00	1.30	15.00	360.00		220.00	150.00		1140.00	380.00	5.70
MEAT												
Bacon, back rasher, raw	7.00	2150.00	0.10	1.00	15.00		120.00	230.00		1470.00		1.60
Bacon, Canadian style	10.80			0.86			295.00	389.00		1545.00		
Bacon, collar, boiled	13.00	1630.00	0.18	1.60	15.00		140.00	170.00		1100.00		3.90
Bacon, gammon, boiled	9.00	1440.00	0.15	1.30	18.00		150.00	210.00		960.00		2.70
Bacon, gammon rasher, grilled/broiled	9.00	3290.00	0.17	1.40	31.00		260.00	480.00		2140.00		3.20
Bacon, rasher, fried	13.00	2970.00	0.12	1.30	20.00		170.00	300.00		1910.00	310.00	2.60
Bacon, rasher, grilled/broiled	12.00	2970.00	0.16	1.50	16.00		160.00	290.00		2020.00		3.00
Bacon, regular	10.50			1.50			336.00	484.00		1594.00		
Bacon, streaky, grilled/broiled	12.00	2930.00	0.15	1.50	16.00		160.00	290.00		1990.00		2.90
Beef, bottom round, cooked	5.80			3.00			255.00	291.00		50.00		
Beef, brisket, boiled	12.00	92.00	0.13	2.80	18.00		150.00	200.00		73.00		6.30
Beef, canned, corned UK style	14.00	1430.00	0.24	2.90	15.00		120.00	140.00		950.00	240.00	5.60

INGREDIENTS per 100g = 3.527oz	CALCIUM mg Ca	CHLORINE mg Cl	COPPER mg Cu	IRON mg Fe	MAGNESIUM mg Mg	MANGANESE mg Mn	PHOSPHORUS mg P	POTASSIUM mg K	SELENIUM mcg Se	SODIUM mg Na	SULPHUR mg S	ZINC mg Zn
Beef, canned, corned US style	20.00			4.30			105.00	60.00		943.00		
Beef, chuck blade pot roast	12.90			2.90			191.00	191.00		62.00		
Beef, dried, chipped	19.00			3.00			398.00	192.00		4241.00		
Beef, forerib, lean roast	13.00	61.00	0.17	2.30	22.00		180.00	310.00		56.00	260.00	6.80
Beef, forerib, roast	14.00	56.00	0.16	1.90	18.00		150.00	260.00		51.00		5.20
Beef, ground	5.80			7.00			250.00	291.00		82.00		
Beef, heart, cooked	6.00			5.90			181.00	232.00		104.00		
Beef, lean only	10.00	65.00	0.19	2.10	22.00		190.00	350.00		59.00	270.00	5.50
Beef, minced, stewed	18.00	470.00	0.24	3.10	20.00		170.00	290.00		320.00	220.00	5.80
Beef, rump steak, grilled/broiled	7.00	61.00	0.18	3.40	25.00		220.00	380.00		55.00		4.90
Beef, silverside, boiled	10.00	65.00	0.19	2.10	22.00		190.00	350.00		59.00	270.00	5.50
Beef, sirloin, grilled/broiled	10.50			3.00			218.00	360.00		62.00		
Beef, sirloin, lean grilled/broiled	11.00			3.30			244.00	402.00		66.60		
Beef, sirloin, roast	10.00	64.00	0.18	1.90	19.00		170.00	300.00		54.00		4.60
Beef, stewed	15.00	550.00	0.25	3.00	21.00		160.00	230.00		360.00		8.70
Beef, topside, roast	6.00	51.00	0.13	2.60	23.00		200.00	350.00		48.00		4.90
Chicken, leg quarter	6.00	54.00	0.07	0.50	15.00		130.00	190.00		50.00	190.00	0.90
Chicken, roast	9.00	87.00	0.12	0.80	24.00		210.00	310.00		81.00	260.00	1.50
Chicken, wing	5.00	44.00	0.06	0.40	12.00		110.00	160.00		41.00	130.00	0.80

INGREDIENTS per 100g = 3.527oz	CALCIUM mg Ca	CHLORINE mg Cl	COPPER mg Cu	IRON mg Fe	MAG-NESIUM mg Mg	MANGA-NESE mg Mn	PHOSPHO-RUS mg P	POT-ASSIUM mg K	SELE-NIUM mcg Se	SODIUM mg Na	SULPHUR mg S	ZINC mg Zn
Duck, roast	12.00	75.00	0.27	2.70	16.00		150.00	210.00		76.00		1.80
Goose, roast	10.00	160.00	0.49	4.60	31.00		270.00	410.00		150.00	320.00	
Grouse, roast	28.00	59.00	0.22	4.60	22.00		190.00	240.00		60.00	240.00	
Ham	9.00	1670.00		1.20	18.00		280.00	280.00		1250.00	180.00	2.30
Hare, stewed	21.00	74.00		10.80	22.00		250.00	210.00		40.00	320.00	
Kidney, ox, stewed	16.00	520.00	0.66	8.00	19.00		300.00	180.00		400.00	270.00	3.00
Kidney, pig, stewed	13.00	480.00	0.84	6.40	21.00		330.00	190.00		370.00		4.70
Kidney, lamb, fried	13.00	330.00	0.65	12.00	29.00		360.00	340.00		270.00	290.00	4.10
Lamb, breast, roast	10.00	74.00	0.19	1.50	18.00		150.00	250.00		73.00		3.60
Lamb, chop, grilled/broiled	7.00	65.00	0.13	1.50	19.00		160.00	250.00		56.00		2.70
Lamb, cutlets, grilled/broiled	9.00	82.00	0.18	1.90	23.00		200.00	320.00		71.00		
Lamb, leg, roast	8.00	62.00	0.28	2.50	25.00		200.00	310.00		65.00		3.30
Lamb, rib, roast	22.00			1.60			163.00	263.00		70.50		4.60
Lamb, scrag end neck, stewed	9.00	340.00	0.22	2.20	18.00		190.00	190.00		240.00		
Lamb, shoulder, roast	9.00	60.00	0.15	1.60	19.00		150.00	260.00		61.00		6.10
Liver, beef, fried	10.50		12.00	6.00			461.00	363.00		105.00		4.30
Liver, calf, fried	15.00	210.00	0.53	7.50	26.00		470.00	410.00		170.00	300.00	6.20
Liver, chicken, fried	15.00	350.00	9.90	9.10	23.00		350.00	290.00		240.00	250.00	3.40
Liver, lamb, fried	12.00	250.00	2.30	10.00	22.00		400.00	300.00		190.00	270.00	4.40
Liver, ox, stewed	11.00	120.00	2.50	7.80	19.00		380.00	250.00		110.00	270.00	4.30
Liver, pig, stewed	11.00	150.00		17.00	22.00		390.00	250.00		130.00	280.00	8.20
Oxtail, stewed	14.00	270.00	0.27	3.80	18.00		140.00	170.00		190.00	290.00	8.80

INGREDIENTS per 100g = 3.527oz	CALCIUM mg Ca	CHLORINE mg Cl	COPPER mg Cu	IRON mg Fe	MAG-NESIUM mg Mg	MANGA-NESE mg Mn	PHOSPHO-RUS mg P	POT-ASSIUM mg K	SELE-NIUM mcg Se	SODIUM mg Na	SULPHUR mg S	ZINC mg Zn
Partridge, roast	46.00	99.00		7.70	36.00		310.00	410.00		100.00	400.00	
Pheasant												
Pigeon, roast	7.00	44.00		8.50	15.00		180.00	180.00		46.00	130.00	
Pork, chop, grilled/broiled	11.00	79.00	0.17	1.20	26.00		230.00	380.00		84.00		2.90
Pork, leg, roast	10.00	79.00	0.25	1.30	22.00		200.00	350.00		79.00		2.90
Pork, pan fried	4.40			0.78			213.00	362.00		69.00		
Pork, rib, roast	10.50			0.90			223.00	368.00		43.00		
Pork, shoulder, braised	7.00			1.60			190.00	336.00		88.00		
Rabbit, stewed	11.00	43.00		1.90	22.00		200.00	210.00		32.00	250.00	
Sweetbread, lamb, fried	34.00	260.00	0.22	1.80	23.00		420.00	260.00		210.00	160.00	2.10
Tongue, ox, boiled	31.00	1450.00		3.00	16.00		230.00	150.00		1000.00	200.00	
Tongue, sheep, stewed	11.00	80.00		3.40	13.00		200.00	110.00		80.00	190.00	
Turkey, gizzard, cooked								149.00		51.00		
Turkey, meat and skin, roast	9.00	47.00	0.14	0.90	24.00		200.00	280.00		52.00		2.10
Turkey, white meat only	7.00	42.00	0.14	0.50	29.00		230.00	340.00		45.00	280.00	1.50
Veal, cutlets, fried in breadcrumbs	10.00	120.00		1.60	33.00		280.00	420.00		110.00	330.00	
Veal, cutlets, grilled/broiled	10.50			0.94			230.00	303.00		65.80		
Veal, fillet, roast	14.00	110.00		1.60	28.00		360.00	430.00		97.00	330.00	

INGREDIENTS
per 100g = 3.527oz

	CALCIUM mg Ca	CHLORINE mg Cl	COPPER mg Cu	IRON mg Fe	MAGNESIUM mg Mg	MANGANESE mg Mn	PHOSPHORUS mg P	POTASSIUM mg K	SELENIUM mcg Se	SODIUM mg Na	SULPHUR mg S	ZINC mg Zn
Veal, jellied	15.00	1650.00	0.34	1.50	19.00		180.00	240.00		1190.00	230.00	3.30
Veal, rib, roast	11.70			0.80			248.00	304.00		67.00		
Venison, haunch, roast	29.00	89.00	0.07	7.80	33.00		290.00	360.00		86.00	320.00	
DAIRY												
Butter	15.00	1150.00	0.03	0.20	2.00	TR	24.00	15.00		750.00	9.00	0.10
Cheese, Brie	540.00	1060.00	TR	0.80	27.00	TR	390.00	100.00		700.00		2.20
Cheese, Camembert	350.00	1120.00	0.07	0.20	21.00	TR	310.00	100.00		650.00		2.70
Cheese, Cheddar/hard	720.00	1030.00	0.03	0.30	25.00	TR	490.00	77.00	12.00	670.00	230.00	2.30
Cheese, Cheshire	560.00	830.00	0.13	0.30	19.00	TR	400.00	87.00	11.00	550.00	230.00	3.30
Cheese, cottage, plain	73.00	550.00	0.04	0.10	9.00	TR	160.00	89.00	4.00	380.00		0.60
Cheese, cream	98.00	480.00	0.04	0.10	10.00	TR	100.00	160.00	1.00	300.00		0.50
Cheese, Danish blue	500.00	1950.00	0.08	0.20	27.00	TR	370.00	89.00	2.00	1260.00		2.00
Cheese, Edam	770.00	1570.00	0.05	0.40	39.00	TR	530.00	97.00		1020.00		2.20
Cheese, Feta, sheep and goat	360.00	2350.00	0.07	0.20	20.00	TR	280.00	95.00		1440.00		0.90
Cheese, full fat, soft	110.00	600.00	0.10	0.10	9.00	TR	130.00	150.00	3.00	330.00		0.70
Cheese, goats' milk, soft	190.00	830.00	TR	0.10	14.00	TR	210.00	130.00		470.00		0.70
Cheese, Gouda	740.00	1440.00	TR	0.10	38.00	TR	490.00	91.00		910.00		1.80
Cheese, Mozzarella	590.00	990.00	TR	0.30	27.00	TR	420.00	75.00		610.00		1.40
Cheese, Parmesan	1200.00	1820.00	0.33	1.10	45.00	0.10	810.00	110.00	11.00	1090.00	250.00	5.30
Cheese, quark	120.00	110.00	0.06	TR	11.00	TR	200.00	140.00		45.00	110.00	0.90
Cheese, ricotta	240.00			0.40	13.00	TR	170.00	110.00		100.00		1.30

INGREDIENTS per 100g = 3.527oz	CALCIUM mg Ca	CHLORINE mg Cl	COPPER mg Cu	IRON mg Fe	MAG-NESIUM mg Mg	MANGA-NESE mg Mn	PHOSPHO-RUS mg P	POT-ASSIUM mg K	SELE-NIUM mcg Se	SODIUM mg Na	SULPHUR mg S	ZINC mg Zn
Cheese, Rocquefort	530.00	2670.00	0.09	0.40	33.00	TR	400.00	91.00		1670.00		1.60
Cheese, Stilton	320.00	1410.00	0.18	0.30	20.00	TR	310.00	130.00	11.00	930.00	230.00	2.50
Cheese, vegetarian Cheddar	690.00	990.00	TR	0.20	31.00	0.10	490.00	67.00	12.00	670.00		1.90
Cream, clotted	37.00	40.00	0.09	0.10	5.00	TR	40.00	55.00	TR	18.00	15.00	0.20
Cream, double	50.00	51.00	TR	0.20	6.00	TR	50.00	65.00	TR	37.00	16.00	0.20
Cream, single	91.00	80.00	TR	0.10	9.00	TR	76.00	120.00	TR	49.00	24.00	0.50
Cream, soured	93.00	81.00	TR	0.40	10.00	TR	81.00	110.00	TR	41.00	27.00	0.50
Cream, whipping	62.00	59.00	TR	TR	7.00	TR	58.00	80.00	TR	40.00	22.00	0.30
Egg, battery	59.00	160.00	0.08	2.00	12.00	TR	200.00	130.00	11.00	140.00	180.00	1.30
Egg, dried	220.00	620.00	0.31	7.30	46.00	0.10	770.00	500.00	42.00	540.00	690.00	5.00
Egg, duck	63.00		0.50	2.90	16.00	0.10	200.00	190.00		120.00		1.40
Egg, free range	59.00	160.00	0.08	2.00	12.00	TR	200.00	130.00	11.00	140.00	180.00	1.30
Egg, quail	64.00			3.70			230.00					
Egg, turkey	99.00			4.10			170.00					
Egg, white	5.00	170.00	0.02	0.10	11.00	TR	33.00	150.00	6.00	190.00	180.00	0.10
Egg, yolk	130.00	140.00	0.15	6.10	15.00	0.10	500.00	120.00	20.00	50.00	170.00	3.90
Milk, dried, skimmed	1280.00	1070.00	TR	0.27	130.00	TR	970.00	1590.00	11.00	550.00	320.00	4.00
Milk, dried, whole	1020.00	810.00	0.02	0.40	84.00	TR	740.00	1270.00	8.00	440.00	240.00	3.20
Milk, goats'	100.00	150.00	0.03	0.12	13.00	TR	90.00	170.00		42.00		0.50
Milk, human, mature	34.00	42.00	0.04	0.07	3.00	TR	15.00	58.00	1.00	15.00	14.00	0.30
Milk, semi-skimmed	120.00	100.00	TR	0.05	11.00	TR	95.00	150.00	1.00	55.00	31.00	0.40
Milk, sheeps'	170.00	82.00	0.10	0.03	18.00	TR	150.00	120.00		44.00		0.70
Milk, skimmed, pasteurized	120.00	100.00	TR	0.05	12.00	TR	95.00	150.00	1.00	50.00	31.00	0.40

INGREDIENTS per 100g = 3.527oz	CALCIUM mg Ca	CHLORINE mg Cl	COPPER mg Cu	IRON mg Fe	MAG-NESIUM mg Mg	MANGA-NESE mg Mn	PHOSPHO-RUS mg P	POT-ASSIUM mg K	SELE-NIUM mcg Se	SODIUM mg Na	SULPHUR mg S	ZINC mg Zn
Milk, skimmed, sterilized	120.00	100.00	0.01	0.09	12.00	TR	95.00	140.00	1.00	54.00	31.00	0.40
Milk, whole	115.00	100.00	TR	0.06	11.00	TR	92.00	140.00	1.00	55.00	30.00	0.40
Whey, dried	646.00			1.40			589.00					
Whey, fluid	51.00			0.10			53.00					
Yoghurt, goats' plain	120.00	130.00	0.01	0.20	14.00	TR	110.00	170.00		39.00		0.40

SOYA PRODUCTS

INGREDIENTS per 100g = 3.527oz	CALCIUM mg Ca	CHLORINE mg Cl	COPPER mg Cu	IRON mg Fe	MAG-NESIUM mg Mg	MANGA-NESE mg Mn	PHOSPHO-RUS mg P	POT-ASSIUM mg K	SELE-NIUM mcg Se	SODIUM mg Na	SULPHUR mg S	ZINC mg Zn
Soya, cheese	450.00	870.00	TR	1.10	29.00	0.10	350.00	130.00		600.00		1.80
Soya, milk	13.00	15.00	0.06	0.40	15.00	0.10	47.00	120.00		32.00		0.20
Soya, milk, powder	275.00											
Soya, Miso	66.00		0.43	2.74	42.00	0.86	153.00	164.00		3647.00		3.32
Soya, Natto	217.00		0.67	8.60	115.00	1.50	174.00	729.00		7.00		3.03
Soya, Tempeh	93.00		0.67	2.26	70.00	1.43	206.00	367.00		6.00		1.81
Tofu	507.00		1.70	1.20	23.00			63.00		4.00		0.70

BEANS, GRAIN AND FLOUR

INGREDIENTS per 100g = 3.527oz	CALCIUM mg Ca	CHLORINE mg Cl	COPPER mg Cu	IRON mg Fe	MAG-NESIUM mg Mg	MANGA-NESE mg Mn	PHOSPHO-RUS mg P	POT-ASSIUM mg K	SELE-NIUM mcg Se	SODIUM mg Na	SULPHUR mg S	ZINC mg Zn
Amaranth	267.00			3.90			67.00	411.00				
Barley, light, pearled	16.00			2.00			189.00	160.00		3.00		
Barley, pot, dry	39.00			2.70			290.00	296.00				
Beans, black, dry	27.00			1.60			139.00	355.00		0.58		
Beans, blackeye, boiled	24.00			2.10			146.00	379.00		1.00		
Beans, blackeye, dry	110.00			6.50	53.00			688.00		6.00		

INGREDIENTS per 100g = 3.527oz	CALCIUM mg Ca	CHLORINE mg Cl	COPPER mg Cu	IRON mg Fe	MAG-NESIUM mg Mg	MANGA-NESE mg Mn	PHOSPHO-RUS mg P	POT-ASSIUM mg K	SELE-NIUM mcg Se	SODIUM mg Na	SULPHUR mg S	ZINC mg Zn
Beans, blackeye, frozen, boiled	25.00											
Beans, butter, boiled	19.00	2.00	0.16	1.70	33.00		87.00	400.00		16.00	47.00	1.00
Beans, butter, dry	85.00	47.00	1.22	5.90	164.00		320.00	1700.00		62.00	110.00	2.80
Beans, Great Northern, boiled	50.00			2.70			147.00	416.00		7.20		
Beans, Great Northern, dry	50.00			2.70			147.00	416.00		7.20		
Beans, haricot, boiled	65.00	1.00	0.14	2.50	45.00		120.00	320.00		15.00	46.00	1.00
Beans, haricot, dry	180.00	2.00	0.61	6.70	180.00		310.00	1160.00		43.00	170.00	2.80
Beans, lima, boiled	47.00			2.50			121.00	422.00		1.00		
Beans, lima, canned	26.10			2.40			66.80	221.00		236.00		
Beans, lima, dry	28.90			3.00			154.00	612.00		2.00		
Beans, mung, dry	100.00	12.00	0.97	8.00	170.00		330.00	850.00		28.00	190.00	
Beans, pea/navy, boiled	50.00			2.70			147.00	416.00		7.20		
Beans, pea/navy, dry	50.00			2.60			147.00	415.00		6.80		
Beans, pinto, canned	37.00		0.14	1.61	27.00	27.00	92.00	301.00		416.00		0.69
Beans, pinto, dry	48.00			3.00			164.00	490.00		1.60		
Beans, red kidney, boiled	38.00			2.40			140.00	340.00		0.30		
Beans, red kidney, canned	24.00		0.15	1.26	28.00	0.24	94.00	257.00		341.00		0.55
Beans, red kidney, dry	140.00	2.00	0.61	6.70	180.00		410.00	1160.00		40.00	170.00	2.80
Beans, soya, boiled	68.00			1.70			309.00	334.00		2950.00		

INGREDIENTS per 100g = 3.527oz	CALCIUM mg Ca	CHLORINE mg Cl	COPPER mg Cu	IRON mg Fe	MAG-NESIUM mg Mg	MANGA-NESE mg Mn	PHOSPHO-RUS mg P	POT-ASSIUM mg K	SELE-NIUM mcg Se	SODIUM mg Na	SULPHUR mg S	ZINC mg Zn
Beans, soya, canned	67.00			2.80			144.00			236.00		
Beans, soya, raw	226.00			8.40	265.00			1677.00		5.00		
Bran, oat			0.48	4.50								3.80
Bran, wheat	110.00	150.00	1.34	2.90	520.00	9.00	1200.00	1160.00		28.00	65.00	16.20
Bread, cracked wheat	64.90			2.60			127.90	133.00		433.00		
Bread, cracked wheat, toasted	76.00			3.30			152.00	161.00		504.70		
Bread, French/Vienna	109.90			3.08			85.00	89.00		579.00		
Bread, pumpernickel	70.90			2.70			218.00	433.00		542.00		
Bread, rye	79.90			2.70			144.90	203.90		0.69		
Bread, rye, toasted	90.00			3.18			163.00	231.00		795.00		
Bread, wholewheat	54.00	880.00	0.26	2.70	76.00	1.90	200.00	230.00	35.00	550.00	81.00	1.80
Bread, wholewheat, toasted	76.00			0.33			152.00	161.90		504.00		
Breadcrumbs	122.00			4.10			141.00	152.00		736.00		
Buckwheat	12.00		0.70	2.00	48.00	1.60	150.00	220.00	9.00	1.00		2.60
Bulgur wheat, dry	28.80			5.50			338.00	228.00		4.00		
Chick pea/garbanzo, boiled	64.00		0.33	3.10	67.00		130.00	400.00		850.00	84.00	
Chick pea/garbanzo, dried	140.00	60.00	0.76	6.40	160.00		183.00	800.00		40.00		
Corn, tortillas	140.00			2.00				143.00		3.30		
Corn/maize meal	18.00			3.30			255.00	284.00		1.00		
Flour, buckwheat	11.00			1.00			87.70	320.00		2.00		
Flour, buckwheat, dark	35.90			2.70			346.90	320.00				

INGREDIENTS per 100g = 3.527oz

Ingredient	CALCIUM mg Ca	CHLORINE mg Cl	COPPER mg Cu	IRON mg Fe	MAG-NESIUM mg Mg	MANGA-NESE mg Mn	PHOSPHO-RUS mg P	POT-ASSIUM mg K	SELE-NIUM mcg Se	SODIUM mg Na	SULPHUR mg S	ZINC mg Zn
Flour, buckwheat, light	11.20			1.00			87.70					
Flour, carob	279.00			4.00			72.80	910.00		17.00		
Flour, corn/maize, dry	6.00			1.10			99.00	120.00				
Flour, lima bean												
Flour, rye	32.00		0.42	2.70	92.00	0.68	360.00	410.00		1.00		3.00
Flour, soya, full fat	210.00	110.00	2.92	6.90	240.00	2.30	600.00	1660.00	9.00	9.00		3.90
Flour, soya, low fat	240.00		3.12	9.10	290.00	2.90	640.00	2030.00	11.00	14.00		3.20
Flour, wheat, wholemeal	38.00	38.00	0.40	3.90	120.00	3.14	320.00	340.00		3.00		2.90
Hominy/corn, grits, dry	4.00			2.90			73.00	80.00		1.00		
Lentils, boiled	13.00	20.00	0.19	2.40	25.00		77.00	210.00		12.00	39.00	1.00
Lentils, raw	39.00	64.00	0.58	7.60	77.00		240.00	670.00		36.00	120.00	3.10
Millet, flour	40.00						260.00	370.00		21.00		
Millet, whole, dry	20.00			6.80			311.00	430.00				
Oatmeal	55.00	73.00	0.23	4.10	110.00	3.70	380.00	370.00	3.00	33.00	160.00	3.00
Oats, rolled, boiled	9.00			0.60			57.00	61.00		218.00		
Oats, rolled, dried	53.00			4.50			405.00	352.00		2.00		
Peas, dried	61.00	60.00	0.49	4.70	116.00		300.00	990.00		38.00	130.00	3.50
Peas, dried, boiled	24.00	9.00	0.17	1.40	30.00		110.00	270.00		13.00	39.00	1.00
Peas, split, dried	33.00	56.00	0.58	5.40	130.00		270.00	910.00		38.00	170.00	4.00
Peas, split, dried, boiled	11.00	10.00	0.25	1.70	30.00	8.00	120.00	270.00		14.00	46.00	1.20
Popcorn, popped	3.00			1.00			73.00	250.00		TR		
Quinoa, dry												
Rice, bran	76.00			19.40			1386.00	1495.00				

INGREDIENTS
per 100g = 3.527oz

	CALCIUM mg Ca	CHLORINE mg Cl	COPPER mg Cu	IRON mg Fe	MAGNESIUM mg Mg	MANGANESE mg Mn	PHOSPHORUS mg P	POTASSIUM mg K	SELENIUM mcg Se	SODIUM mg Na	SULPHUR mg S	ZINC mg Zn
Rice, brown, boiled	4.00	91.00	0.33	0.50	43.00	0.90	120.00	99.00		1.00	36.00	0.70
Rice, brown, raw	10.00	230.00	0.85	1.40	110.00	2.00	310.00	250.00	TR	3.00	90.00	1.80
Rice, wild	19.00			4.20			339.00	220.00		7.00		
Rye, wholegrain	38.00			3.70			376.00	467.00		1.00		
Sago	10.00	13.00	0.03	1.20	3.00		29.00	5.00		3.00	1.00	
Sorghum, grain	28.00			4.40			287.00	350.00				
Tapioca, dry	0.40			0.40			18.00	18.00		0.30		
Wheat, durum	37.00			4.30			386.00	386.00		3.00		
Wheatgerm	55.00	80.00	0.90	8.50	270	12.30	1050.00	950.00	3.00	5.00	250.00	17.00

OILS
Almond
Apricot kernel
Cocoa butter
Coconut
Cod liver
Corn
Cottonseed
Grapeseed
Hazelnut
Linseed
Olive
Palm
Palm kernel
Peanut

INGREDIENTS
per 100g = 3.527oz

	CALCIUM mg Ca	CHLORINE mg Cl	COPPER mg Cu	IRON mg Fe	MAGNESIUM mg Mg	MANGANESE mg Mn	PHOSPHORUS mg P	POTASSIUM mg K	SELENIUM mcg Se	SODIUM mg Na	SULPHUR mg S	ZINC mg Zn
Poppyseed												
Ricebran												
Safflower												
Sesame												
Soyabean												
Soyabean lecithin												
Sunflower												
Walnut												
Wheatgerm												
CONDIMENTS												
Arrowroot	7.00	7.00	0.22	2.00	8.00		27.00	18.00		5.00	2.00	
Baking powder	11300.00	29.00	TR	TR	9.00		8430.00	49.00		11800.00		
Barmene	25.00	59.00	0.07	0.40	15.00		32.00	300.00		84.00		0.04
Dill pickle	26.00			1.00			21.00	200.00		1427.00		
Fructose												
Ginger root, fresh	36.00			2.10			5.90	264.00		6.00		
Honey	5.00			0.50				50.00		5.00		
Honeycomb	8.00	26.00	0.04	0.20	2.00		32.00	35.00		7.00	1.00	
Honey, in jar	5.00	18.00	0.05	0.40	2.00		17.00	51.00		11.00	1.00	
Marmite	95.00		0.30	3.70	180.00		1700.00	2600.00		4500.00		2.10
Molasses, blackstrap	684.00			16.10			84.00					
Mustard, prepared	80.00			2.00			80.00	140.00		1260.00		
Salt		6600.00		TR				TR		3876.00		
Tahini	254.00						54.00					

INGREDIENTS
per 100g = 3.527oz

	CALCIUM mg Ca	CHLORINE mg Cl	COPPER mg Cu	IRON mg Fe	MANGANESE mg Mn	MAGNESIUM mg Mg	PHOSPHORUS mg P	POTASSIUM mg K	SELENIUM mcg Se	SODIUM mg Na	SULPHUR mg S	ZINC mg Zn
Tamari										5160.00		
Vecon	6.00			70.00			9.00	130.00		900.00		24.00
Vinegar, cider apple	15.00	47.00	0.04	0.60				100.00		1.00		
Vinegar, malt				0.50			32.00	89.00		20.00	19.00	
Vinegar, white wine	9.00					22.00	49.00	49.00				
HERBS												
Basil, ground	2113.00			42.00		422.00	490.00	3433.00		34.00		
Bay leaf, powdered	834.00			43.00		120.00	113.00	529.00		23.00		
Chervil, dried	1346.00			31.95		130.00	450.00	4740.00		83.00		8.80
Chives, fresh	66.00			0.30			33.00	266.00				
Dill weed, fresh	1784.00			48.77		451.00	543.00	3308.00		208.00		3.30
Marjoram, dried	1990.00			82.71		346.00	306.00	1522.00		77.00		3.60
Oregano, dried	1576.00			44.00		270.00	200.00	1669.00		15.00		4.43
Parsley, dried	1568.00			97.86		249.00	351.00	3805.00		452.00		4.75
Parsley, fresh	203.00			6.00			63.00	726.00		45.00		
Rosemary, dried	1280.00			29.30		220.00	70.00	955.00		50.00		3.20
Sage, ground	1652.00			28.12		428.00	91.00	1070.00		11.00		4.70
Savory, ground	2132.00			37.88		377.00	140.00	1051.00		24.00		4.30
Tarragon, ground	1139.00			32.30		347.00	313.00	3020.00		62.00		3.90
Thyme, ground	1890.00			123.60		220.00	201.00	814.00		55.00		6.18
NUTS												
Almond	233.00			4.70			504.00	773.00		4.20		
Brazil	178.00			3.50			607.00	607.00		3.50		

INGREDIENTS per 100g = 3.527oz

	CALCIUM mg Ca	CHLORINE mg Cl	COPPER mg Cu	IRON mg Fe	MAGNESIUM mg Mg	MANGANESE mg Mn	PHOSPHORUS mg P	POTASSIUM mg K	SELENIUM mcg Se	SODIUM mg Na	SULPHUR mg S	ZINC mg Zn
Cashew	45.00		2.20	6.00	260.00		490.00	565.00		16.00		5.60
Chestnut, dried	52.00			3.30			875.00	875.00		12.00		
Chestnut, raw	27.00			1.70			88.00	454.00		6.00		
Hazel/Filbert	44.00	6.00	0.21	1.10	56.00		230.00	350.00		1.00	75.00	2.40
Hickory	TR			2.40			360.00					
Macadamia	48.00			2.00			161.00	264.00				
Peanut	72.00			2.20			406.00	700.00		4.86		
Peanut butter	37.00	500.00	0.70	2.10	180.00		330.00	700.00		350.00		3.00
Pecan	36.00			2.00			290.00	391.00		0.90		
Pine/Piñon	7.00			3.00			35.00	635.00		71.00		
Pistachio	130.00			7.20			499.00	971.00				
Walnut, black	57.00			3.00			471.00	532.00		TR		
Walnut, English	96.00			2.50			321.00	507.00		10.00		

SEEDS

	CALCIUM mg Ca	CHLORINE mg Cl	COPPER mg Cu	IRON mg Fe	MAGNESIUM mg Mg	MANGANESE mg Mn	PHOSPHORUS mg P	POTASSIUM mg K	SELENIUM mcg Se	SODIUM mg Na	SULPHUR mg S	ZINC mg Zn
Linseed/Linquist Gold	0.48		1.82	12.00	0.72			1.90		0.04		39.00
Melon	50.00			8.00								
Poppy	1448.00			9.40	331.00		848.00	700.00		21.00		
Pumpkin	42.00			15.00			1189.00	817.00		17.80		10.23
Safflower	78.00						644.00					
Sesame	137.00			7.50			775.00	412.00		37.00		
Sunflower	117.00			6.70			714.00	696.00		3.50		

SPICES

	CALCIUM mg Ca	CHLORINE mg Cl	COPPER mg Cu	IRON mg Fe	MAGNESIUM mg Mg	MANGANESE mg Mn	PHOSPHORUS mg P	POTASSIUM mg K	SELENIUM mcg Se	SODIUM mg Na	SULPHUR mg S	ZINC mg Zn
Allspice	661.00			7.06	135.00		113.00	1044.00		77.00		1.01

INGREDIENTS per 100g = 3.527oz	CALCIUM mg Ca	CHLORINE mg Cl	COPPER mg Cu	IRON mg Fe	MANGANESE mg Mn	MAGNESIUM mg Mg	PHOSPHORUS mg P	POTASSIUM mg K	SELENIUM mcg Se	SODIUM mg Na	SULPHUR mg S	ZINC mg Zn
Aniseed	646.00			36.96		170.00	440.00	1441.00		16.00		5.30
Asafoetida	690.00			22.20								
Caraway	689.00			16.23		258.00	568.00	1351.00		17.00		5.50
Cardamom pod, ground	383.00			13.97		229.00	178.00	1119.00		18.00		7.47
Celery	1750.00			4.50			550.00	1400.00		150.00		
Chili, powder	278.00			14.25		170.00	303.00	1916.00		1010.00		2.70
Cinnamon	1217.00			39.00			43.00	521.00		43.00		
Cloves, ground	646.00			8.86		264.00	105.00	1102.00		243.00		1.09
Coriander, leaves, dried	1246.00			42.50		694.00	481.00	4466.00		211.00		
Coriander, seed	709.00			16.32		330.00	409.00	1267.00		35.00		4.70
Cumin, seed	931.00			66.35		366.00	499.00	1788.00		168.00		4.80
Curry leaves, raw	811.00			3.10								
Curry powder	478.00			29.59		254.00	349.00	1543.00		52.00		4.05
Dill, seed	1516.00			16.32		256.00	277.00	1186.00		20.00		5.20
Fennel, seed	1196.00			18.54		385.00	487.00	1694.00		88.00		3.70
Fenugreek, seed	176.00			33.53		191.00	296.00	770.00		67.00		2.50
Garlic, powder	71.00			3.50			428.00	1107.00		35.00		
Ginger, ground	116.00			11.52		184.00	148.00	1342.00		32.00		4.72
Mustard, powder	330.00	62.00		10.90		260.00	180.00	940.00		5.00	1280.00	6.50
Mustard, seed	521.00		0.20	9.98		298.00	841.00	682.00		5.00		5.70
Nutmeg, powder	184.00			3.00		183.00	213.00	350.00		16.00		2.15
Onion, powder	380.00			4.70			333.00	952.00		47.00		
Paprika	177.00			23.60		185.00	345.00	2344.00		34.00		4.10

INGREDIENTS
per 100g = 3.527oz

	CALCIUM mg Ca	CHLORINE mg Cl	COPPER mg Cu	IRON mg Fe	MAG-NESIUM mg Mg	MANGA-NESE mg Mn	PHOSPHO-RUS mg P	POT-ASSIUM mg K	SELE-NIUM mcg Se	SODIUM mg Na	SULPHUR mg S	ZINC mg Zn
Pepper, black	428.00			28.50			190.00	1238.00		47.00		
Pepper, cayenne	148.00			7.80	152.00		293.00	2014.00		30.00		2.48
Pepper, white	265.00			14.31	90.00		176.00	73.00		5.00		1.13
Saffron	111.00			11.10			252.00	1724.00		148.00		
Turmeric	182.00			41.40	193.00		268.00	2525.00		38.00		4.40
Yeast, bakers, dried	212.00			17.50			1750.00	1900.00		125.00		
Yeast, brewers	212.00			17.50			1750.00	1900.00		125.00		
Yeast, brewers debittered	210.00			17.30			1754.00	1894.00		121.00		
Yeast, torula	424.00			19.30			1713.00	2046.00		15.00		

TABLE 3: Vitamin and trace element content

INGREDIENTS per 100g = 3.527oz	VITAMIN A RE mcg	VITAMIN B1 mg	VITAMIN B2 mg	VITAMIN B3 mg	VITAMIN B6 mg	VITAMIN B12 mcg	VITAMIN C mg	VITAMIN D mcg	VITAMIN E mg	VITAMIN K mg	BIOTIN mcg	FOLIC ACID mcg	PANTO-THENIC ACID mg
VEGETABLES													
Alfalfa leaf concentrate*	6500.00	0.20	0.25	10.90	0.45				12IU	0.45	22.00	0.15	2.00
Alfalfa sprouts	15.00	0.09	0.12	0.60			9.00						
Arrowhead	0.00	0.16	0.04	1.40			5.00						
Artichoke, globe, boiled	14.00	0.05	0.04	0.59	0.08	0.00	7.40	0.00	0.20			44.50	0.20
Artichoke, Jerusalem, boiled	0.00	0.10	TR			0.00	2.00	0.00	0.20				
Artichoke, Jerusalem, raw	2.00	0.20	0.06	1.30			4.00						
Arvi/colocasia root	4.00	0.08	0.03	1.60			3.00	0.00				54.00	
Asparagus, boiled	83.00	0.09	0.12	1.05	0.14	0.00	27.10					98.10	0.16
Aubergine/eggplant, boiled	6.25	0.07	0.02	0.60			1.00						
Aubergine/eggplant, raw	0.00	0.05	0.03	0.80	0.08	0.00	5.00	0.00				20.00	0.22
Bamboo shoots, canned	1.60	0.15	0.07	0.90			4.00	0.00				7.00	
Bamboo shoots, raw	0.00	0.02	0.05	0.30		0.00	0.00						
Beans, broad, boiled	27.00	0.12	0.09	1.20		0.00	19.80						
Beans, broad, raw	35.00	0.17	0.11	1.50		0.00	33.00						
Beans, French, boiled	66.60	0.04	0.07	0.30	0.06	0.00	5.00	0.00	0.20		0.80	28.00	0.07
Beans, runner, boiled	66.60	0.03	0.07	0.50	0.04	0.00	5.00	0.00	0.20		0.50	28.00	0.04
Beans, runner, raw	66.60	0.05	0.10	0.90	0.07	0.00	20.00	0.00	0.20		0.70	60.00	0.05

INGREDIENTS per 100g = 3.527oz	VITAMIN A RE mcg	VITAMIN B1 mg	VITAMIN B2 mg	VITAMIN B3 mg	VITAMIN B6 mg	VITAMIN B12 mcg	VITAMIN C mg	VITAMIN D mcg	VITAMIN E mg	VITAMIN K mg	BIOTIN mcg	FOLIC ACID mcg	PANTO-THENIC ACID mg
Beans, snap, boiled	66.40	0.11	0.09	0.60			9.00						
Beans, snap, raw	60.00	0.08	0.10	0.54			18.00						
Beansprouts, mung, boiled													
Beansprouts, mung, raw	1.90	0.08	0.12	0.70			13.00						
Beansprouts, soya, boiled													
Beansprouts, soya, raw													
Beetroot, boiled	1.00	0.03	0.01	0.27	0.03	0.00	5.50					53.20	0.09
Beetroot, raw	2.00	0.05	0.02	0.40	0.05	0.00	11.00					92.60	0.15
Beetroot tops, boiled	610.00	0.10	0.22	0.40	0.10	0.00	30.00						0.25
Beetroot tops, raw	610.00	0.10	0.22	0.40	0.11	0.00	30.00						0.25
Bok choy, boiled	310.00	0.04	0.08	0.70			15.00						
Bok choy, raw	310.00	0.05	0.10	0.80			25.00						
Borage	420.00	0.06	0.15	0.90		0.00	35.00						
Broccoli, boiled	141.00	0.08	0.20	0.75	0.19	0.00	62.80					68.40	0.28
Broccoli florets, raw	154.00	0.06	0.11	0.63	0.15	0.00	93.20					71.00	0.53
Brussels sprouts, boiled	66.60	0.06	0.10	0.40	0.17	0.00	40.00	0.00	0.90		0.30	87.00	0.28
Brussels sprouts, raw	66.60	0.10	0.15	0.70	0.28	0.00	90.00	0.00	1.00		0.40	110.00	0.40
Burdock root, boiled	0.00	0.04	0.06	0.32			3.00						
Burdock root, raw	6.00	0.01	0.03	0.30									
Cabbage, red	4.00	0.05	0.03	0.30	0.21	0.00	57.00					20.70	0.32

INGREDIENTS per 100g = 3.527oz	VITAMIN A RE mcg	VITAMIN B1 mg	VITAMIN B2 mg	VITAMIN B3 mg	VITAMIN B6 mg	VITAMIN B12 mcg	VITAMIN C mg	VITAMIN D mcg	VITAMIN E mg	VITAMIN K mg	BIOTIN mcg	FOLIC ACID mcg	PANTOTHENIC ACID mg
Cabbage, savoy, boiled	89.00	0.05	0.09	0.02	0.15	0.00	17.00	0.00				35.00	0.15
Cabbage, savoy, raw	100.00	0.07	0.03	0.30	0.19	0.00	31.00						0.21
Cabbage, spring, boiled	83.30	0.03	0.03	0.20	0.10	0.00	25.00	0.00	0.20		TR	50.00	0.15
Cabbage, white	0.00	0.06	0.05	0.30	0.16	0.00	40.00	0.00	0.20		0.10	26.00	0.21
Cabbage, winter, boiled	50.00	0.03	0.03	0.20	0.10	0.00	20.00	0.00	0.20		TR	35.00	0.15
Cabbage, winter, raw	50.00	0.06	0.05	0.30	0.16	0.00	55.00	0.00	0.20		0.10	90.00	0.21
Cardoon, boiled	12.00	0.01	0.03	0.29		0.00	1.70						
Cardoon, raw	12.00	0.02	0.03	0.30		0.00	2.00						
Carrot, boiled	2000.00	0.05	0.04	0.40	0.09	0.00	4.00	0.00	0.50		0.40	8.00	0.18
Carrot, old, raw	2000.00	0.06	0.05	0.60	0.15	0.00	6.00	0.00	0.50		0.60	15.00	0.25
Carrot, young, boiled	1000.00	0.05	0.04	0.40	0.09	0.00	4.00	0.00	0.50		0.40	8.00	0.18
Cassava	0.00	0.05	0.04	0.60			0.00	0.00	0.00			24.00	
Cauliflower, boiled	1.00	0.06	0.05	0.55	0.20		55.40					51.20	0.12
Cauliflower florets, raw	2.00	0.07	0.05	0.63	0.23	0.00	71.50	0.00				66.10	0.14
Celeriac, boiled	0.00	0.02	0.03	0.42	0.10	0.00	3.60						
Celeriac, raw	0.00	0.05	0.05	0.70	0.17	0.00	8.00						
Celery, boiled	TR	0.03	0.00	0.20	0.06	0.00	10.00		0.20		TR	6.00	0.28
Celery, raw	TR	0.03	0.03	0.30	0.10	0.00	7.00	0.00	0.20		0.10	12.00	0.40
Chayote	2.50	0.01	0.02	0.40		0.00	14.00	0.00					
Chervil							9.00						
Chicory	TR	0.05	0.05	0.50	0.05	0.00	4.00	0.00				52.00	

INGREDIENTS per 100g = 3.527oz	VITAMIN A RE mcg	VITAMIN B1 mg	VITAMIN B2 mg	VITAMIN B3 mg	VITAMIN B6 mg	VITAMIN B12 mcg	VITAMIN C mg	VITAMIN D mcg	VITAMIN E mg	VITAMIN K mg	BIOTIN mcg	FOLIC ACID mcg	PANTO-THENIC ACID mg
Chili, hot	1075.00	0.08	0.08	0.80			242.00						
Chili, red	0.00	0.37	0.51	2.50		0.00	96.00	0.00				16.00	
Chinese leaves	119.00	0.03	0.05	0.39			27.00						
Collard greens, boiled	222.00	0.01	0.04	0.20			10.00						
Corn salad		0.08	0.26	1.00									
Coriander leaves	277.00	0.07	0.12	0.73		0.0	10.50						
Courgette/zucchini	58.30	0.05	0.09	0.40			16.00		0.00			48.00	
Cucumber	TR	0.04	0.04	0.20	0.04	0.0	8.00	0.00	TR		0.40	16.00	0.30
Curly endive	206.00	0.08	0.08	0.40			6.00	0.00					
Dandelion leaves, boiled	1170.00	0.13	0.17	0.40			18.00						
Dandelion leaves, raw	1400.00	0.90	0.20				35.00						
Dock, boiled	347.00	0.03	0.08	0.41		0.0	26.30						
Dock, raw	400.00	0.04	0.10	0.50		0.0	48.00						
Endive	333.30	0.06	0.10	0.40			12.00	0.00				330.00	
Fennel leaves					0.01		31.00						
Garlic	TR	0.24	0.05	0.40		0.00	10.00	0.00				6.00	
Gherkins, pickled	2.00	0.13	0.10	6.00		0.00	6.00	0.00				40.00	
Gherkins, raw	22.80	0.01	0.05	0.20		0.00	11.00	0.00				18.00	
Gourd, bitter	65.30	0.09	0.12	0.40		0.00	184.00	0.00				45.00	
Gourd, bottle	0.16	0.03	0.03	0.40		0.00	10.00	0.00				6.00	
Gourd, ridge	4.80	0.07	0.02	0.40		0.00	3.00	0.00				37.00	
Horseradish	0.00	0.05	0.03	0.50	0.15	0.00	120.00	0.00					
Kale, boiled	740.00	0.05	0.06	0.50									
Kale, raw	1000.00	0.16	0.26	2.10			40.00						

INGREDIENTS per 100g = 3.527oz	VITAMIN A RE mcg	VITAMIN B1 mg	VITAMIN B2 mg	VITAMIN B3 mg	VITAMIN B6 mg	VITAMIN B12 mcg	VITAMIN C mg	VITAMIN D mcg	VITAMIN E mg	VITAMIN K mg	BIOTIN mcg	FOLIC ACID mcg	PANTO-THENIC ACID mg
Kantola	0.00	0.05	0.04	0.30		0.00	189.00	0.00					
Kohlrabi, boiled	4.80	0.04	0.01	0.36			54.00						
Leek, boiled	6.60	0.07	0.03	0.40	0.15	0.00	15.00	0.00	0.80		1.00		0.10
Leek, raw	6.60	0.10	0.05	0.60	0.25	0.00	18.00	0.00	0.80		1.40		0.12
Lettuce, butterhead	97.00	0.06	0.06	0.30			8.00						
Lettuce, cos/romaine	189.00	0.05	0.07	0.35			18.00						
Lettuce, crisphead	29.00	0.03	0.02	0.10			3.20						
Lettuce, iceberg	33.00	0.04	0.03	0.18	0.04	0.00	3.90	0.00					
Lettuce, round	166.60	0.07	0.08	0.30	0.07	0.00	15.00	0.00	0.50		0.70	34.00	0.20
Mangetout, boiled	13.00	0.10	0.06	0.50			48.00						
Mangetout, raw	14.00	0.15	0.08	0.60		0.00	60.00	0.00					
Marrow, boiled	5.00	TR	TR	0.20	0.06	0.00	2.00	0.00	TR			6.00	0.07
Marrow, raw	5.00	TR	TR	0.30	0.06	0.00	5.00	0.00	TR		0.40	13.00	0.10
Marrow, Parwal	30.00	0.06	0.08	0.80			18.00	0.00				29.00	
Mooli	0.00	0.02	0.03	0.70			42.00						
Mushroom, boiled	0.00	0.07	0.30	4.40		0.00	3.80						
Mushroom, raw	0.00	0.10	0.40	4.00	0.10	0.00	3.00	0.00	TR				
Mushroom, Chinese, dried	0.00	0.37	1.32	11.30		0.00	0.00	0.00				23.00	2.00
Mushroom, shiitake, boiled		0.03	0.17	0.50		0.00	0.30	0.00				23.00	
Mushroom, shiitake, dried	0.00	0.30	0.27	14.10		0.00	3.50	0.00	0.70				
Mustard and cress	83.30					0.00	40.00	0.00					
Mustard greens, boiled	302.00	0.04	0.06	0.42		0.00	25.00						

INGREDIENTS per 100g = 3.527oz

INGREDIENTS per 100g = 3.527oz	VITAMIN A RE mcg	VITAMIN B1 mg	VITAMIN B2 mg	VITAMIN B3 mg	VITAMIN B6 mg	VITAMIN B12 mcg	VITAMIN C mg	VITAMIN D mcg	VITAMIN E mg	VITAMIN K mg	BIOTIN mcg	FOLIC ACID mcg	PANTO-THENIC ACID mg
Mustard leaves	436.00	0.03				0.00	33.00	0.00					0.26
Okra	15.00	0.10	0.10	1.00	0.08	0.00	25.00	0.00				100.00	
Okra pod, boiled	57.00	0.12	0.05	0.80			16.00						0.02
Okra pod, raw	49.00	0.13	0.18	0.90			20.00						0.10
Olives, in brine	30.00	TR	TR	TR	0.02	0.00	0.00	0.00			TR		0.14
Onion, boiled	0.00	0.02	0.04	0.10	0.06	0.00	6.00	0.00	TR		0.60	8.00	
Onion, raw	0.00	0.03	0.05	0.20	0.10	0.00	10.00	0.00	TR		0.90	16.00	
Onion, shallot	0.00	0.04	0.05	1.00		0.00	6.00	0.00					
Onion, spring	0.00	0.03	0.05	0.20	0.10	0.00	25.00	0.00	TR		0.90	40.00	0.14
Onion, Welsh		0.50	0.09	0.40			27.00						
Parsnip, boiled	TR	0.07	0.06	0.70	0.06	0.00	10.00	0.00	1.00		TR	30.00	0.35
Parsnip, raw	TR	0.10	0.08	1.00	0.10	0.00	15.00	0.00	1.00		0.10	67.00	0.50
Peas, boiled	50.00	0.25	0.11	1.50	0.10	0.00	15.00	0.00	TR		0.40		0.32
Peas, frozen, boiled	50.00	0.32	0.10	1.50	0.07	0.00	17.00	0.00	TR		0.40	78.00	32.00
Peas, raw	50.00	0.32	0.15	2.50	0.16	0.00	25.00	0.00	TR		0.50		0.75
Pepper, green, boiled	33.30	0.01	0.02	0.60	0.14	0.00	60.00	0.00	0.80			11.00	0.16
Pepper, green, raw	33.30	TR	0.03	0.70	0.17	0.00	100.00	0.00	0.80			11.00	0.23
Potato, baked in skin	TR	0.08	0.03	1.00	0.14	0.00	8.00	0.00	0.10		TR	8.00	
Potato, chipped	TR	0.10	0.04	1.20	0.18	0.00	9.00	0.00	0.10		TR	10.00	0.16
Potato, new, boiled	TR	0.11	0.03	1.20	0.20	0.00	18.00	0.00	0.10		TR	10.00	0.20
Potato, old, boiled	TR	0.08	0.03	0.80	0.18	0.00	9.00	0.00	0.10		TR	10.00	0.20
Pumpkin, boiled	108.00	0.03	0.07	0.40			4.80						0.20
Pumpkin leaves, boiled	247.00	0.06	0.13	0.85		0.00	1.00						

INGREDIENTS per 100g = 3.527oz	VITAMIN A RE mcg	VITAMIN B1 mg	VITAMIN B2 mg	VITAMIN B3 mg	VITAMIN B6 mg	VITAMIN B12 mcg	VITAMIN C mg	VITAMIN D mcg	VITAMIN E mg	VITAMIN K mg	BIOTIN mcg	FOLIC ACID mcg	PANTOTHENIC ACID mg
Purslane, boiled	0.00	0.03	0.09	0.46		0.00	10.50						
Purslane, raw	133.00	0.04	0.11	0.48		0.00	21.00					24.00	0.18
Radish	.TR	0.04	0.02	0.20	0.10	0.00	25.00	0.00	0.00				
Rutabaga, boiled	55.00	0.06	0.06	0.80			26.00						
Rutabaga, raw	0.00	0.09	0.04	0.70	0.10	0.00	25.00						
Salsify, boiled		0.03					4.00	0.00					
Salsify, raw		0.08	0.22	0.50		0.00	8.00						
Sauerkraut, canned	1.60	0.02	0.02	0.12			14.00						
Sea kale, boiled		0.06				0.00	18.00	0.00					
Seaweed, arame, dried	30.00	0.02	0.20	2.60	0.60		0.00						
Seaweed, hijiki, dried	90.00	0.01	0.20	4.00			0.00						
Seaweed, kelp/kombu, dried	320.00	0.07	0.26	2.10		0.00	13.00						
Seaweed, kelp/kombu, raw													
Seaweed, kelp/kombu, soaked		0.03	0.08	0.50			1.00						
Seaweed, nori/laver, dried	10790.00	0.24	1.34	5.50	0.07		14.00						
Seaweed, nori/laver, soaked	10.00	0.05	0.06	0.20									
Seaweed, spirulina, dried	64.00	3.00	3.70	12.80			10.00						
Seaweed, wakame, dried	36.00	0.06	0.23	1.60		0.00	3.00						

INGREDIENTS per 100g = 3.527oz	VITAMIN A RE mcg	VITAMIN B1 mg	VITAMIN B2 mg	VITAMIN B3 mg	VITAMIN B6 mg	VITAMIN B12 mcg	VITAMIN C mg	VITAMIN D mcg	VITAMIN E mg	VITAMIN K mg	BIOTIN mcg	FOLIC ACID mcg	PANTO-THENIC ACID mg
Seaweed, wakame, raw	36.00	0.06	0.23	1.60			3.00						
Sorrel, boiled	1080.00	0.06	0.13	0.30			54.00						
Sorrel, raw	1290.00	0.09	0.22	0.50			119.00						
Spinach, boiled	600.00	0.07	0.15	0.40	0.18	0.00	25.00	0.00	2.00		0.10	140.00	0.21
Spinach, raw	810.00	0.10	0.20	1.40			50.00						
Spinach, New Zealand, boiled	362.00	0.03	0.10	0.39		0.00	16.00						
Spinach, New Zealand, raw	440.00	0.04	0.13	0.50	0.16	0.00	30.00	0.00	1.10		0.40	110.00	0.31
Spring greens, boiled	666.60	0.06	0.20	0.50		0.00	30.00						30.00
Squash, spaghetti, boiled	11.00	0.04	0.02	0.80	0.10	0.00	3.50					8.00	0.35
Squash, spaghetti, raw	5.00	0.03	0.01	0.95	0.10	0.00	2.10					12.00	0.36
Squash, summer, boiled	28.00	0.04	0.03	0.50			5.00						
Squash, winter, boiled	364.00	0.08	0.02	0.68			10.00						
Succotash, boiled	29.00	0.16	0.09	1.32	0.12	0.00	8.20						0.57
Succotash, raw	29.00	0.20	0.08	1.58	0.13	0.00	15.10						0.12
Swede, boiled	TR	0.04	0.03	0.80	0.12	0.00	17.00	0.00	0.00		TR	21.00	0.07
Sweet potato, baked in skin	1727.00	0.70	0.10	0.60			24.00						
Sweet potato, raw	666.60	0.10	0.06	0.80	0.22	0.00	25.00	0.00	4.00			52.00	0.94
Sweetcorn, baby, canned	23.30	0.02	0.04	0.60		0.00	14.00	0.00					

INGREDIENTS per 100g = 3.527oz	VITAMIN A RE mcg	VITAMIN B1 mg	VITAMIN B2 mg	VITAMIN B3 mg	VITAMIN B6 mg	VITAMIN B12 mcg	VITAMIN C mg	VITAMIN D mcg	VITAMIN E mg	VITAMIN K mg	BIOTIN mcg	FOLIC ACID mcg	PANTO-THENIC ACID mg
Sweetcorn, cob, boiled	40.00	0.15	0.08	1.70	0.19	0.00	12.00	0.00	0.80			52.00	0.54
Sweetcorn kernel, canned	33.00	0.03	0.05	1.00			5.00						
Sweetcorn kernel, raw	40.00	0.11	0.10	1.30			7.00						
Swiss chard, boiled	314.00	0.03	0.08	0.36		0.00	18.00						
Swiss chard, raw	330.00	0.04	0.09	0.40		0.00	30.00						0.17
Tomato, canned	83.30	0.06	0.03	0.70	0.11	0.00	18.00	0.00	1.20		1.50	25.00	0.20
Tomato, raw	100.00	0.06	0.04	0.70	0.11	0.00	20.00	0.00	1.20		1.50	28.00	0.33
Tomato, green, raw	27.00						14.00						
Tomato purée	54.00	0.02	0.20	0.68	0.26		27.00						
Turnip greens, boiled	550.00	0.40	0.06	0.40			60.00						
Turnip greens, raw	760.00	0.07	0.10	0.60	0.06	0.00	17.00	0.00	0.00			194.40	0.38
Turnip, boiled	0.00	0.03	0.04	0.40		0.00	15.00	0.00			TR	10.00	0.14
Vine leaves	383.00	0.08	0.24	0.50		0.00		0.00					
Water chestnut, canned	0.70	0.01	0.02	0.30		0.00	1.00						
Water chestnut, raw	0.00	0.08	0.16	0.90		0.00	7.00						
Watercress	500.00	0.10	0.10	0.60	0.13	0.00	60.00	0.00	1.00		0.40		0.10
Yam, boiled	2.00	0.05	0.01	0.50		0.00	2.00	0.00				6.00	0.44
Yam, raw	2.00	0.10	0.03	0.40		0.00	10.00	0.00					0.63

FRUIT

INGREDIENTS per 100g = 3.527oz	VITAMIN A RE mcg	VITAMIN B1 mg	VITAMIN B2 mg	VITAMIN B3 mg	VITAMIN B6 mg	VITAMIN B12 mcg	VITAMIN C mg	VITAMIN D mcg	VITAMIN E mg	VITAMIN K mg	BIOTIN mcg	FOLIC ACID mcg	PANTO-THENIC ACID mg
Acerola		0.02	0.05	0.30			1066.00						
Apple, dried	0.00	0.00	0.15	0.90	0.12	0.00	3.90						

INGREDIENTS per 100g = 3.527oz	VITAMIN A RE mcg	VITAMIN B1 mg	VITAMIN B2 mg	VITAMIN B3 mg	VITAMIN B6 mg	VITAMIN B12 mcg	VITAMIN C mg	VITAMIN D mcg	VITAMIN E mg	VITAMIN K mg	BIOTIN mcg	FOLIC ACID mcg	PANTO-THENIC ACID mg
Apple, cooking, baked in skin	3.00	0.03	0.01	0.10	0.01	0.00	10.00	0.00	0.10		0.20	2.00	0.06
Apple, eating, peeled	3.00	0.04	0.02	0.10	0.03	0.00	3.00	0.00	0.20		0.30	5.00	0.10
Apple butter	0.00	0.01	0.02	0.20			2.00						
Apple juice, concentrate													
Apricot, canned in water	182.00	0.02	0.02	0.39	0.04	0.00	3.90	0.00					
Apricot, boiled	210.00	0.03	0.04	0.40	0.17	0.00	5.00	0.00				2.00	0.23
Apricot, dried	600.00	TR	0.20	3.00	0.05	0.00	TR	0.00				10.30	0.70
Apricot, dried, boiled	221.00	TR	0.06	1.10	0.07	0.00	TR	0.00				2.00	0.23
Apricot, raw	250.00	0.04	0.05	0.60		0.00	7.00	0.00				5.00	0.30
Avocado	16.00	0.10	0.10	1.00	0.42	0.00	15.00		3.20		3.20	66.00	1.07
Banana, dried	31.00	0.18	0.24	2.80		0.00	7.00						
Banana, raw	33.00	0.04	0.07	0.60	0.51	0.00	10.00	0.00	0.20			14.00	0.26
Banana flakes, dehydrated	76.00	0.18	0.24	2.80		0.00							
Bilberry	21.00	0.02	0.02	0.40	0.06	0.00	7.00	0.00				6.00	0.16
Blackberry, boiled	14.00	0.03	0.03	0.03	0.03	0.00	22.00	0.00	3.00		0.30		0.19
Blackberry, raw	16.60	0.03	0.04	0.04	0.05	0.00	15.00	0.00	3.50		0.40		0.25
Breadfruit	4.00	0.11	0.03	0.90			20.00						
Cherimoya	0.59	0.05	0.06	0.74			5.20						
Cherry, cooking	20.00	0.05	0.07	0.30	0.05	0.00	5.00	0.00	0.10		0.40	8.00	0.26
Cherry, eating	20.00	0.05	0.07	0.30	0.05	0.00	5.00	0.00	0.10		0.40	6.00	0.26
Coconut, creamed	0.00	0.03	TR	0.90		0.00	3.00	0.00					

INGREDIENTS per 100g = 3.527oz	VITAMIN A RE mcg	VITAMIN B1 mg	VITAMIN B2 mg	VITAMIN B3 mg	VITAMIN B6 mg	VITAMIN B12 mcg	VITAMIN C mg	VITAMIN D mcg	VITAMIN E mg	VITAMIN K mg	BIOTIN mcg	FOLIC ACID mcg	PANTO-THENIC ACID mg
Coconut, desiccated	0.00	0.06	0.10	0.60	0.30		1.50					9.00	0.80
Coconut flesh	0.00	0.04	0.02	0.44			2.20						0.22
Coconut water/milk	0.00	TR	TR	0.10			2.00						0.31
Crabapple	4.00	0.03	0.02	0.10	0.04	0.00	8.00	0.00					0.10
Cranberry	3.00	0.03	0.02	0.10		0.00	12.00	0.00			2.10	2.00	0.40
Currant, black, boiled	28.00	0.03	0.05	0.30	0.06	0.00	150.00	0.00	0.90		2.40		0.05
Currant, black, dried	4.20	0.03	0.08	0.50	0.30	0.00	0.00	0.00			2.20	11.00	0.05
Currant, black, raw	33.00	0.03	0.06	0.30	0.08	0.00	200.00	0.00	1.00		2.20		0.05
Currant, red, boiled	10.00	0.03	0.05	0.10	0.03	0.00	31.00	0.00	0.10		2.20		0.06
Currant, red, raw	11.00	0.04	0.06	0.10	0.03	0.00	40.00	0.00	0.10		2.60		
Currant, white, boiled	TR	0.03	0.05	0.10	0.03	0.00	31.00	0.00	0.10				
Currant, white, raw	TR	0.04	0.06	0.10	0.05	0.00	40.00	0.00	0.10				
Damson, boiled, no stone	30.00	0.08	0.03	0.30	0.03	0.00	3.00	0.00	0.50		0.10	1.00	0.21
Date, dried, no stone	8.30	0.07	0.04	2.00	0.15	0.00	0.00	0.00				21.00	0.80
Elderberry	60.00	0.07	0.06	0.50	0.23	0.00	36.00	0.00					0.14
Fig, dried	8.30	0.10	0.08	1.70	0.18	0.00	0.00	0.00				9.00	0.43
Fig, dried, stewed	5.00	0.05	0.04	0.90	0.08	0.00	0.00	0.00				2.00	0.22
Fig, raw	83.00	0.06	0.05	0.40	0.11	0.00	2.00	0.00					0.30
Gooseberry, ripe, raw	30.00	0.04	0.03	0.30	0.02	0.00	40.00	0.00	0.40		0.10		0.30
Gooseberry, stewed	25.00	0.03	0.03	0.30	0.02	0.00	31.00	0.00	0.30		0.40		0.12
Granadilla	37.00	TR	0.05	0.85			14.00						
Grapefruit, flesh	12.00	0.03	0.02	0.25	0.04	0.00	34.40	0.00	0.30			10.20	0.28
Grapefruit, pink, Florida	26.00	0.04	0.02	0.20	0.04	0.00	37.00	0.00	0.30			9.40	0.28

INGREDIENTS per 100g = 3.527oz	VITAMIN A RE mcg	VITAMIN B1 mg	VITAMIN B2 mg	VITAMIN B3 mg	VITAMIN B6 mg	VITAMIN B12 mc	VITAMIN C mg	VITAMIN D mcg	VITAMIN E mg	VITAMIN K mg	BIOTIN mcg	FOLIC ACID mcg	PANTO-THENIC ACID mg
Grape, black, flesh	TR	0.04	0.02	0.30	0.10	0.00	4.00	0.00			0.30	6.00	0.05
Grape, black, whole	TR	0.03	0.02	0.20	0.08	0.00	3.00	0.00			0.20	5.00	0.04
Grape, white, flesh	TR	0.04	0.02	0.30	0.10	0.00	4.00	0.00			0.30	6.00	0.05
Grape, white, whole	TR	0.04	0.02	0.30			TR	0.00	4.00				
Greengage, raw, no stone	0.00	0.05	0.03	0.40	0.05	0.00	3.00	0.00	0.70		TR	3.00	0.20
Guava, flesh	79.00	0.05	0.05	1.20	0.14	0.00	183.00	0.00					0.15
Jujube	4.00	0.02	0.04	0.90			98.00						
Kiwifruit, peeled	18.00	0.02	0.05	0.50			37.40				0.50		0.23
Kumquat	30.00	0.08	0.10			0.00							
Lemon, whole	TR	0.05	0.04	0.20	0.10	0.00	80.00				0.30	7.00	0.10
Lemon juice, fresh	TR	0.02	0.01	0.10	0.05	0.00	50.00					8.20	0.21
Lime, whole	1.00	0.03	0.02	0.20	0.04	0.00	29.00	0.00	0.00				0.13
Lime juice, fresh	1.00	0.02	0.01	0.10	0.04	0.00	29.00						
Loganberry, stewed	12.50	0.02	0.03	0.40	0.05	0.00	29.00	0.00	0.30				0.20
Loganberry, whole	13.30	0.02	0.03	0.40	0.06	0.00	35.00	0.00	0.30				0.24
Loquat	153.00	0.01	0.02	0.18		0.00	1.00	0.00			0.00		0.04
Lychee	TR	0.04	0.04	0.30	0.10	0.00	40.00	0.00					
Mango	389.00	0.05	0.05	0.58	0.10	0.00	27.00	0.00					0.16
Melon, cantaloupe	333.00	0.05	0.03	0.50	0.07	0.00	25.00	0.00	0.10			30.00	0.23
Melon, honeydew, flesh	16.60	0.05	0.03	0.50	0.07	0.00	25.00	0.00	0.10			30.00	0.23
Melon, water, flesh	3.00	0.02	0.02	0.20	0.07	0.00	5.00	0.00	0.10			3.00	1.55
Mulberry	3.00	0.02	0.10	0.60		0.00	36.00	0.00					
Nectarine	74.00	0.01	0.04	0.90	0.03	0.00	5.40	0.00				3.70	0.15

INGREDIENTS per 100g = 3.527oz	VITAMIN A RE mcg	VITAMIN B1 mg	VITAMIN B2 mg	VITAMIN B3 mg	VITAMIN B6 mg	VITAMIN B12 mcg	VITAMIN C mg	VITAMIN D mcg	VITAMIN E mg	VITAMIN K mg	BIOTIN mcg	FOLIC ACID mcg	PANTO-THENIC ACID mg
Orange, whole	25.00	0.10	0.05	0.50	0.09	0.00	71.00	0.00	0.20				0.33
Orange juice, fresh	8.00	0.10	0.02	0.28	0.05	0.00	32.90	0.00				18.10	0.19
Orange, Florida, flesh	20.00	0.10	0.04	0.40	0.05	0.00	45.00	0.00				17.30	0.25
Ortanique	12.00	0.10	0.04	0.40		0.00	50.00	0.00					
Papaya, no stone	201.00	0.02	0.03	0.33	0.01	0.00	61.80						0.21
Passionfruit	1.60	TR	0.10	1.50		0.00	20.00	0.00					
Peach, dried	216.00	0.02	212.00	4.30	0.06	0.00	4.80	0.00					
Peach, dried, stewed	123.00	TR	0.06	2.00	0.06	0.00	0.10	0.00	TR			2.00	10.00
Peach, flesh and skin	83.00	0.02	0.05	1.00	0.02	0.00	8.00	0.00			0.20	3.00	0.15
Pear, dried	0.00	0.00	0.14	1.30		0.00	7.00						
Pear, raw	2.00	0.02	0.04	0.10	0.01	0.00	4.00	0.00				7.30	0.07
Pear, stewed	1.50	0.03	0.03	0.20	0.02	0.00	3.00	0.00	TR		0.10	5.00	0.05
Persimmon						0.00	66.00					7.50	
Pineapple, flesh	2.00	0.09	0.03	0.40	0.08	0.00	15.40	0.00				10.60	0.16
Plantain, boiled	10.00	TR	0.01	0.30	0.30	0.00	3.00	0.00				18.00	0.26
Plantain, raw	10.00	0.05	0.70	0.70	0.50	0.00	20.00	0.00				16.00	0.37
Plum, stewed, no stone	30.00	0.04	0.03	0.50	0.03	0.00	3.00	0.00	0.50		TR	1.00	0.12
Plum, raw, flesh	36.00	0.05	0.03	0.50	0.05	0.00	3.00	0.00	0.70		TR	3.00	0.15
Pomegranate, raw		0.03	0.03	0.30	0.10	0.00	6.10	0.00					0.59
Pomegranate juice	0.00	0.02	0.03	0.20		0.00	8.00	0.00					
Pricklypear	5.00	0.01	0.06	0.46		0.00	14.00						
Prune, dried, no stone	199.00	0.08	0.16	1.90	0.26	0.00	3.30					3.70	0.46
Prune, stewed	31.00	0.02	0.10	0.70	0.22	0.00	2.90	0.00				0.10	0.11
Quince	4.00	0.02	0.03	0.20	0.04	0.00	15.00	0.00					0.08

INGREDIENTS per 100g = 3.527oz	VITAMIN A RE mcg	VITAMIN B1 mg	VITAMIN B2 mg	VITAMIN B3 mg	VITAMIN B6 mg	VITAMIN B12 mcg	VITAMIN C mg	VITAMIN D mcg	VITAMIN E mg	VITAMIN K mg	BIOTIN mcg	FOLIC ACID mcg	PANTOTHENIC ACID mg
Raisin	5.00	0.10	0.08	0.50	0.30	0.00	0.00					4.00	0.10
Raspberry, raw	13.30	0.02	0.03	0.40	0.06	0.00	25.00		0.30		1.90		0.24
Raspberry, stewed	14.00	0.02	0.03	0.40	0.05	0.00	23.00	0.00	0.30		2.00		0.23
Rhubarb, stewed	9.00	TR	0.03	0.30	0.02	0.00	8.00	0.00	0.20			4.00	0.06
Sapodilla/Naseberry	4.00	TR	TR	0.20		0.00	13.00	0.00					
Sapotes	6.80	0.01	0.02	1.80	0.06	41.00	20.00						
Strawberry	5.00	0.02	0.03	0.40	0.06	0.00	60.00	0.00	0.20		1.10	20.00	0.34
Sultana/golden raisin	5.00	0.10	0.08	0.50	0.30	0.00	0.00		0.70			4.00	10.00
Tangerine, peeled	92.00	0.11	0.02	0.16	0.06	0.00	30.80	0.00				20.40	0.20
FISH													
Abalone, canned	105.00	0.01	0.04	2.60									
Anchovy, canned in oil	62.00	TR	0.10	3.80		11.00						18.00	
Bloater, grilled/broiled	49.00	TR	0.18	4.00	0.57	11.00	TR	25.00	0.30		10.00	10.00	0.88
Caviar, sturgeon, granular													
Clam, canned	13.00	0.02	0.06	2.60			9.00						
Clam, meat	26.00	0.09	0.15	1.10		TR	TR	TR					
Cockles, boiled								TR					
Cod, dried, salted, raw													
Cod, fillet, raw	TR	0.08	0.07	1.70	0.33	2.00	TR	TR	0.44		3.00	12.00	0.20
Cod, steak, frozen	TR	0.06	0.05	1.50	0.38	2.00	TR	TR			3.00	12.00	0.20
Cod Roe, hard, raw	140.00	1.50	1.00	1.50	0.32	10.00	30.00	2.00	6.40		13.00		30.00
Coley	TR	0.10	0.20	3.40	0.47	4.00	TR	TR	0.36		7.00		0.38

INGREDIENTS per 100g = 3.527oz	VITAMIN A RE mcg	VITAMIN B1 mg	VITAMIN B2 mg	VITAMIN B3 mg	VITAMIN B6 mg	VITAMIN B12 mcg	VITAMIN C mg	VITAMIN D mcg	VITAMIN E mg	VITAMIN K mg	BIOTIN mcg	FOLIC ACID mcg	PANTO-THENIC ACID mg
Crab, boiled	TR	0.10	0.15	2.50			TR	TR					
Crab, canned	TR	TR	0.05	1.10		TR	TR	TR			TR		
Cuttlefish	0.00	0.05		6.10		1.00	0.00					13.00	0.15
Eel, raw	1200.00	0.20	0.35	3.50	0.30	1.00	TR						
Eel, smoked													
Eel, stewed	1900.00	0.13	0.40	2.80	0.24	1.00	TR						0.17
Flounder, baked with lemon	35.00	0.05	0.08	1.60			1.00						
Frogs' legs	0.00	0.14	0.25	1.20									
Haddock, fillet, steamed	TR	0.8	0.13	5.10	0.25	1.00	TR	TR			6.00	16.00	0.20
Haddock, Finnan		0.06	0.05	2.10									
Haddock, fresh, raw	TR	0.07	0.10	4.00	0.20	1.00	TR	TR			5.00	13.00	0.20
Haddock, smoked, steamed	TR	0.10	0.11	1.70	0.35	3.00	4.40				3.00	5.00	0.20
Halibut, grilled/broiled	174.00	0.07	0.08	9.00			1.00	TR	TR				
Halibut, raw	TR	0.08	0.10	5.00	0.20	1.00		TR	0.90		5.00	12.00	0.30
Halibut, steamed	TR	0.08	0.11	5.20	0.23	1.00		TR	1.00		5.00	14.00	0.28
Herring, grilled/broiled	49.00	TR	0.18	4.00			TR	25.00	0.30				
Herring, pickled	38.00	0.04	0.18	2.80			0.00						
Herring, raw	45.00	TR	0.18	4.10	0.45	6.00	TR	22.50	0.21		10.00	5.00	1.00
Herring, roe, soft, raw			0.20	0.50	5.00	5.00	2.00		2.50				0.49
Hilsa				2.80			24.00	25.00					
Kipper, baked	49.00	TR	0.18	4.00	0.57	11.00	TR	25.00	0.30		10.00	10.00	0.88

INGREDIENTS per 100g = 3.527oz	VITAMIN A RE mcg	VITAMIN B1 mg	VITAMIN B2 mg	VITAMIN B3 mg	VITAMIN B6 mg	VITAMIN B12 mcg	VITAMIN C mg	VITAMIN D mcg	VITAMIN E mg	VITAMIN K mg	BIOTIN mcg	FOLIC ACID mcg	PANTO-THENIC ACID mg
Ling Cod	0.00	0.05	0.04										
Lobster. boiled	TR	0.08	0.05	1.50		1.00	TR	TR	1.50		5.00	17.00	1.63
Mackerel. canned	43.00	0.06	0.21	5.80									
Mackerel. fried	52.00	0.09	0.38	8.70	0.84	12.00	TR	21.10			8.00		0.96
Mackerel. raw	45.00	0.09	0.35	8.00	0.70	10.00	TR	17.50			7.00		1.00
Mackerel. smoked													
Mussels. boiled							TR		1.20				
Ocean Perch. breaded. fried	23.00	0.11	0.12	2.30									
Octopus	5.00	0.12	0.11	7.90			0.00						
Oysters, breaded, fried	97.00	0.15	0.22	2.80			8.80						
Oysters, raw	75.00	0.10	0.20	1.50	0.03	15.00	TR	TR	0.85		10.00	10.00	0.50
Pilchard. canned in tomato	TR	0.02	0.29	7.60		12.00	TR	8.00					
Plaice, raw	TR	0.30	0.10	3.20	0.43	2.00	TR	TR	0.70			10.00	0.80
Plaice, steamed	TR	0.30	0.11	3.20	0.47	2.00	TR	TR				11.00	0.70
Prawns. boiled	TR						TR	TR					
Prawns, dried	0.00	0.16	0.34	9.50		12.00	0.00						
Prawns, fresh, raw	20.00	0.04	0.08	5.30		1.00	1.00					2.00	
Red Snapper, raw		0.06	0.11	4.70									
Salmon, pink, canned	21.00	0.03	0.17	8.00			0.00						
Salmon, raw	TR	0.20	0.15	7.00	0.75		TR	TR	1.50		5.00	26.00	2.00
Salmon, red, baked	87.00	0.18	0.14	5.50		5.00							
Salmon, red, canned	90.00	0.04	0.18	7.00	0.45	4.00	TR	12.50			5.00	12.00	0.50
Salmon. smoked	TR	0.16	0.17	8.80			TR	TR					

INGREDIENTS per 100g = 3.527oz

Ingredient	VITAMIN A RE mcg	VITAMIN B1 mg	VITAMIN B2 mg	VITAMIN B3 mg	VITAMIN B6 mg	VITAMIN B12 mcg	VITAMIN C mg	VITAMIN D mcg	VITAMIN E mg	VITAMIN K mg	BIOTIN mcg	FOLIC ACID mcg	PANTOTHENIC ACID mg
Salmon, steamed	TR	0.20	0.11	7.00	0.83	6.00	TR	TR			4.00	29.00	1.80
Sardine, canned in oil	TR	0.04	0.36	8.20	0.48	28.00	TR	7.50	0.30		5.00	8.00	0.50
Sardine, canned in tomato	TR	0.02	0.28	5.50	0.35	14.00	TR	7.50	0.51		5.00	13.00	0.50
Scallop, steamed	TR	0.08	0.05	1.30			TR	TR			5.00	17.00	0.14
Scampi, fried	TR	0.03	0.03	3.00			TR	TR			.TR		
Shrimps, boiled	TR	0.03	0.07	2.80	0.10	1.00	TR	TR			1.00		
Shrimps, dried		0.06	0.09	2.80								70.00	0.30
Shrimps, fried		TR	0.02	0.50		4.90	0.00						
Shrimps, frozen	26.00	0.02	0.08	2.00		2.60						14.00	
Skate, fried		0.09	0.08	2.00			TR		1.00				
Sole, Lemon, raw	TR	0.09	0.09	3.50		1.00	TR	TR			5.00	11.00	0.30
Sole, Lemon, steamed	TR	0.09	0.11	3.60		1.00	TR	TR			5.00	13.00	0.31
Sprats, dried		TR	0.11	3.00								15.00	
Sprats, fresh, raw	20.00	0.04	0.31	7.50		6.90							
Sprats, fried				6.80			TR						
Squid, dried		0.13	0.17	5.30			0.00						
Squid, fresh, raw	15.00	0.03	0.08	2.10		1.30	0.00						
Squid, frozen, raw		0.05	0.02			2.50	0.00					2.00	
Trout, grilled/broiled with butter	70.00	0.08	0.08	2.70	0.44	5.00	1.00						
Tuna, canned in oil		0.04	0.11	12.90			TR	5.80	6.30		3.00	15.00	0.42
Tuna, canned in water		0.03	0.10	15.00			0.00						
Tuna, raw	37.00						TR		0.80				
Whelks, boiled							TR	TR					

INGREDIENTS per 100g = 3.527oz	VITAMIN A RE mcg	VITAMIN B1 mg	VITAMIN B2 mg	VITAMIN B3 mg	VITAMIN B6 mg	VITAMIN B12 mcg	VITAMIN C mg	VITAMIN D mcg	VITAMIN E mg	VITAMIN K mg	BIOTIN mcg	FOLIC ACID mcg	PANTO-THENIC ACID mg
Whitebait, fried	TR						TR						
Whiting, steamed							TR	TR					
Winkles, boiled							TR	TR					
MEAT													
Bacon, back rasher, raw	TR	0.35	0.14	3.10	0.26	TR	0.00	TR	0.07		1.00	2.00	0.40
Bacon, Canadian style	0.00	0.82	0.19	6.90	0.24	TR	0.00		0.14		2.00	TR	0.40
Bacon, collar, boiled	TR	0.27	0.22	2.60	0.26	TR	0.00	TR	0.11		2.00	TR	0.40
Bacon, gammon, boiled	TR	0.44	0.15	3.40		TR	0.00	TR					
Bacon, gammon rasher, grilled/broiled	TR	0.88	0.24	6.30	0.33	TR	0.00	TR	0.07		3.00	2.00	0.60
Bacon, rasher, fried	TR	0.41	0.21	5.20	0.30	TR	0.00	TR	0.18		3.00	1.00	0.30
Bacon, rasher, grilled/broiled	TR	0.43	0.17	4.50	0.27	TR	0.00	TR	0.11		2.00	1.00	0.50
Bacon, regular	0.00	0.68	0.26	7.30			0.00						
Bacon, streaky, grilled/broiled	TR	0.40	0.16	4.20	0.25	TR	0.00	TR	0.12		2.00	2.00	0.50
Beef, bottom round, cooked	TR	0.07	0.22	3.80			0.00						
Beef, brisket, boiled	TR	0.04	0.30	4.30	0.23	1.00	0.00	TR	0.35		TR	7.00	0.50
Beef, canned, corned UK style	TR	TR	0.23	2.50	0.06	2.00	0.00	TR	0.78		2.00	2.00	0.40

INGREDIENTS per 100g = 3.527oz	VITAMIN A RE mcg	VITAMIN B1 mg	VITAMIN B2 mg	VITAMIN B3 mg	VITAMIN B6 mg	VITAMIN B12 mcg	VITAMIN C mg	VITAMIN D mcg	VITAMIN E mg	VITAMIN K mg	BIOTIN mcg	FOLIC ACID mcg	PANTO-THENIC ACID mg
Beef, canned, corned US style	TR	0.02	0.20	3.40			0.00						
Beef, chuck blade pot roast		0.07	0.22	2.30			0.00						
Beef, dried, chipped	TR	0.06	0.30	3.75			0.00						
Beef, forerib, lean roast	TR	0.05	0.33	5.50	0.33	2.00	0.00	TR	0.29		TR	17.00	0.90
Beef, forerib, roast	TR	0.04	0.24	3.90	0.24	1.00	0.00	TR	0.36		TR	13.00	0.60
Beef, ground	TR	0.14	0.18	5.00			0.00						
Beef, heart, cooked	30.00	0.25	1.22	7.60			1.00						
Beef, lean only	TR	0.07	0.31	6.00	0.33	2.00	0.00	TR	0.29		TR	17.00	0.90
Beef, minced, stewed	TR	0.05	0.33	4.40	0.30	2.00	0.00	TR	0.31		TR	16.00	0.80
Beef, rump steak, grilled/broiled	TR	0.08	0.32	5.70	0.29	2.00	0.00	TR	0.32		TR	15.00	0.80
Beef, silverside, boiled	TR	0.03	0.27	3.30	0.28	2.00	0.00	TR	0.33		TR	15.00	0.80
Beef, sirloin, grilled/broiled	TR	0.11	0.27	3.80			0.00						
Beef, sirloin, lean grilled/broiled	TR	0.12	0.30	4.30			0.00						
Beef, sirloin, roast													
Beef, stewed	TR	0.03	0.33	3.60	0.30	2.00	0.00	TR	0.31		TR	16.00	0.80
Beef, topside, roast	TR	0.07	0.31	5.70	0.29	2.00	0.00	TR	0.32		TR	15.00	0.80
Chicken, leg quarter	TR	0.05	0.12	5.10	0.16	TR	0.00	TR	0.07		2.00	6.00	0.70
Chicken, roast	TR	0.08	0.19	8.20	0.26	TR	0.00	TR	0.11		3.00	10.00	1.20
Chicken, wing	TR	0.04	0.10	4.10	0.13	TR	0.00	TR	0.06		2.00	5.00	0.60

INGREDIENTS per 100g = 3.527oz	VITAMIN A RE mcg	VITAMIN B1 mg	VITAMIN B2 mg	VITAMIN B3 mg	VITAMIN B6 mg	VITAMIN B12 mcg	VITAMIN C mg	VITAMIN D mcg	VITAMIN E mg	VITAMIN K mg	BIOTIN mcg	FOLIC ACID mcg	PANTO-THENIC ACID mg
Duck, roast													
Goose, roast													
Grouse, roast													
Ham	TR	0.52	0.25	3.90	0.22	.TR	0.00	TR	0.08		1.00	TR	0.60
Hare, stewed													
Kidney, ox, stewed	250.00	0.25	2.10	4.80	0.28	15.00	10.00		0.42		53.00	43.00	2.40
Kidney, pig, stewed	140.00	0.19	2.10	6.10	0.30		11.00		0.36				
Kidney, lamb, fried	160.00	0.56	2.30	9.60	0.13	79.00	9.00		0.41			5.10	42.00
Lamb, breast, roast	TR	0.06	0.17	3.40	0.12	1.00	0.00	TR	0.13		1.00	3.00	0.40
Lamb, chop, grilled/broiled	TR	0.09	0.16	4.00	0.15	2.00	0.00	TR	0.09		1.00	2.00	0.40
Lamb, cutlets, grilled/broiled	TR	0.10	0.20	4.80	0.18		0.00						
Lamb, leg, roast	TR	0.12	0.31	5.40	0.19	2.00	0.00	TR	0.13		1.00	3.00	0.50
Lamb, rib, roast	TR	0.09	0.21	6.40	0.16	2.00	0.00	TR	0.11		1.00	3.00	0.60
Lamb, scrag end neck, stewed	TR	0.04	0.18	2.70		2.00	27.00	TR	0.11		1.00	4.00	0.60
Lamb, shoulder, roast	TR	0.07	0.20	3.10		2.00	0.00	TR	0.12		1.00	3.00	0.50
Liver, beef, fried	9120.00	0.20	4.00	14.00		87.00	0.00		0.05		53.00	320.00	8.80
Liver, calf, fried	17416.00	0.27	4.20	15.60	0.73	49.00	13.00	0.25	0.34		170.00	500.00	5.50
Liver, chicken, fried	11116.00	0.37	1.70	10.50	0.45	81.00	13.00	0.50	0.32		41.00	240.00	7.60
Liver, lamb, fried	20610.00	0.26	4.40	15.20	0.49	110.00	12.00	1.13	0.44		50.00	290.00	5.70
Liver, ox, stewed	20356.00	0.18	3.60	10.30	0.52	3.00	15.00	1.13	0.16		1.00	7.00	1.00
Liver, pig, stewed	11600.00	0.21	3.10	11.50	0.27	2.00	9.00	TR	0.45			9.00	0.90
Oxtail, stewed	TR	0.02	0.28	3.30	0.14		0.00				2.00		

INGREDIENTS per 100g = 3.527oz	VITAMIN A RE mcg	VITAMIN B1 mg	VITAMIN B2 mg	VITAMIN B3 mg	VITAMIN B6 mg	VITAMIN B12 mcg	VITAMIN C mg	VITAMIN D mcg	VITAMIN E mg	VITAMIN K mg	BIOTIN mcg	FOLIC ACID mcg	PANTO-THENIC ACID mg
Partridge, roast													
Pheasant													
Pigeon, roast				3.90			0.00						
Pork, chop, grilled/broiled	TR	0.66	0.20	5.70	0.31	1.00	0.00	TR	0.03		2.00	6.00	1.00
Pork, leg, roast	TR	0.65	0.27	5.00	0.31	1.00	0.00	TR	0.03		2.00	6.00	1.00
Pork, pan fried	3.00	1.00	0.26	5.00			TR						
Pork, rib, roast	3.00	0.58	0.28	4.90			TR						
Pork, shoulder, braised	3.50	0.54	0.30	5.00			TR						
Rabbit, stewed		0.07	0.28	8.50	0.50	12.00	0.00				1.00	4.00	0.80
Sweetbread, lamb, fried	TR	0.03	0.24	2.10	0.02	4.00	18.00	TR	1.20		5.00	14.00	0.80
Tongue, ox, boiled	TR	0.06	0.29	4.10	0.09	4.00	2.00	TR	0.35		3.00	5.00	0.50
Tongue, sheep, stewed	TR	0.13	0.45	3.70	0.10	7.00	6.00	TR	0.32		2.00	4.00	0.80
Turkey, gizzard, cooked		0.03	0.14	5.80									
Turkey, meat and skin, roast							0.00						
Turkey, white meat only	TR	0.07	0.14	10.00	0.31	1.00	0.00	TR	0.02		1.00	13.00	0.80
Veal, cutlets, fried in breadcrumbs	TR					1.00	0.00	TR			TR		
Veal, cutlets, grilled/broiled	TR	0.07	0.24	5.40			0.00						
Veal, fillet, roast	TR	0.06	0.27	7.00	0.32	1.00	0.00	TR			TR	4.00	0.05

INGREDIENTS per 100g = 3.527oz	VITAMIN A RE mcg	VITAMIN B1 mg	VITAMIN B2 mg	VITAMIN B3 mg	VITAMIN B6 mg	VITAMIN B12 mcg	VITAMIN C mg	VITAMIN D mcg	VITAMIN E mg	VITAMIN K mg	BIOTIN mcg	FOLIC ACID mcg	PANTO-THENIC ACID mg
Veal, jellied	TR	0.05	0.29	6.00	0.14	2.00	0.00	TR	0.12		3.00	3.00	0.30
Veal, rib, roast	TR	0.12	0.30	7.70			0.00						
Venison, haunch, roast		0.22					0.00						
DAIRY													
Butter	886.00	TR	0.02	0.01	TR	TR	TR	0.76	2.00		TR	TR	0.04
Cheese, Brie	320.00	0.04	0.43	0.43	0.15	1.20	TR	0.20	0.84		5.60	58.00	0.35
Cheese, Camembert	282.00	0.05	0.52	0.96	0.22	1.10	TR	0.18	0.65		7.60	102.00	0.36
Cheese, Cheddar/hard	362.00	0.03	0.40	0.07	0.10	1.10	TR	0.26	0.53		3.00	33.00	0.36
Cheese, Cheshire	386.00	0.03	0.48	0.11	0.09	0.90	TR	0.24	0.70		4.00	40.00	0.31
Cheese, cottage, plain	45.60	0.03	0.26	0.13	0.08	0.70	TR	0.03	0.08		3.00	27.00	0.40
Cheese, cream	421.00	0.06	0.73	0.04	0.04	0.30	TR	0.27	1.00		1.60	11.00	0.27
Cheese, Danish blue	321.00	0.03	0.41	0.48	0.12	1.00	TR	0.23	0.76		2.70	50.00	0.53
Cheese, Edam	200.00	0.03	0.35	0.07	0.09	2.10	TR	19.00	0.48		1.80	40.00	0.38
Cheese, Feta, sheep and goat	225.00	0.19	0.21	0.19	0.07	1.10	TR	0.50	0.37		2.40	23.00	0.36
Cheese, full fat, soft		0.03	0.17	0.07	0.05	0.30	TR				2.00	13.00	0.31
Cheese, goats' milk, soft	310.00	0.04	0.63	0.65	0.12	2.00	TR	0.50	0.79			19.00	
Cheese, Gouda	269.00	0.03	0.30	0.05	0.08	1.70	TR	0.24	0.53		1.40	43.00	0.32
Cheese, Mozzarella	268.00	0.03	0.31	0.08	0.09	2.10	TR	0.16	0.33		2.20	19.00	0.25
Cheese, Parmesan	380.00	0.03	0.44	0.12	0.13	1.90	TR	0.25	0.70		3.30	12.00	0.43
Cheese, quark	2.00	0.04	0.30	0.19	0.08	0.70	1.00	TR	TR		3.00	45.00	0.44
Cheese, ricotta	200.00	0.02	0.19	0.09	0.03	0.30	TR	TR	0.03				

INGREDIENTS per 100g = 3.527oz	VITAMIN A RE mcg	VITAMIN B1 mg	VITAMIN B2 mg	VITAMIN B3 mg	VITAMIN B6 mg	VITAMIN B12 mcg	VITAMIN C mg	VITAMIN D mcg	VITAMIN E mg	VITAMIN K mg	BIOTIN mcg	FOLIC ACID mcg	PANTO-THENIC ACID mg
Cheese, Rocquefort	296.00	0.04	0.65	0.57	0.09	0.40	TR		0.55		2.30	45.00	0.50
Cheese, Stilton	385.00	0.03	0.43	0.49	0.16	1.00	TR	0.27	0.61		3.60	77.00	0.71
Cheese, vegetarian Cheddar	461.00	0.03	0.45	0.04	0.11	1.20	TR	0.27	0.80		2.60	25.00	0.46
Cream, clotted	819.00	0.02	0.16	0.04	0.03	0.10	TR	0.28	1.48		1.00	6.00	0.14
Cream, double	654.00	0.02	0.16	0.04	0.03	0.20	1.00	0.27	1.10		1.10	7.00	0.19
Cream, single	347.00	0.04	0.17	0.07	0.05	0.30	1.00	0.14	0.40		1.80	7.00	0.28
Cream, soured	347.00	0.03	0.17	0.07	0.04	0.20	TR	0.15	0.44		1.50	12.00	0.24
Cream, whipping	609.00	0.02	0.17	0.04	0.04	0.20	1.00	0.22	0.86		1.40	7.00	0.22
Egg, battery	190.00	0.09	0.47	0.07	0.12	2.40	0.00		1.11		20.00	51.00	1.74
Egg, dried	730.00	0.31	1.81	0.27	0.46	7.20	0.00	6.75	4.28		69.40	190.00	6.90
Egg, duck	560.00	0.16	0.47	0.17	0.25	5.40	0.00	1.88				80.00	
Egg, free range	190.00	0.09	0.47	0.07	0.12	2.40	0.00	1.75	1.11		20.00	51.00	1.74
Egg, quail		0.13	0.79	0.15	0.15		0.00						
Egg, turkey		0.11	0.47	0.02			0.00						
Egg, white	0.00	0.01	0.43	0.09	0.02	0.10	0.00	0.00	0.00		7.00	13.00	0.30
Egg, yolk	535.00	0.30	0.54	0.06	0.30	6.90	0.00	4.94	3.11		50.00	130.00	4.60
Milk, dried, skimmed	350.00	0.38	1.63	1.02	0.60	2.60	13.00	2.10	0.27		20.10	51.00	3.28
Milk, dried, whole	318.00	0.31	1.40	0.60	0.48	2.40	9.00	0.24	0.61		13.90	46.00	2.79
Milk, goats'	44.00	0.04	0.13	0.31	0.06	0.10	1.00	0.11	0.03		3.00	1.00	0.41
Milk, human, mature	62.00	0.34	0.03	0.22	0.01	0.01	4.00	0.04	0.34		0.70	5.00	0.25
Milk, semi-skimmed	TR	0.04	0.18	0.09	0.06	0.04	1.00	0.01	0.03		2.00	6.00	0.32
Milk, sheeps'	83.00	0.08	0.32	0.41	0.08	0.60	5.00	0.18	0.11		2.50	5.00	0.45
Milk, skimmed, pasteurized	1.00	0.04	0.18	0.09	0.06	0.40	1.00	TR	TR		2.00	6.00	0.32

INGREDIENTS per 100g = 3.527oz

	VITAMIN A RE mcg	VITAMIN B1 mg	VITAMIN B2 mg	VITAMIN B3 mg	VITAMIN B6 mg	VITAMIN B12 mcg	VITAMIN C mg	VITAMIN D mcg	VITAMIN E mg	VITAMIN K mg	BIOTIN mcg	FOLIC ACID mcg	PANTO-THENIC ACID mg
Milk, skimmed, sterilized	1.00	0.03	0.14	0.10	0.04	0.1	TR	TR	TR		2.00	TR	0.32
Milk, whole	55.00	0.03	0.18	0.09	0.06	0.5	1.00	0.03	0.03		2.00	6.00	0.32
Whey, dried	5.00	0.50	2.51	0.80									
Whey, fluid	1.00	0.03	0.14	0.10									
Yoghurt, goats' plain	TR	0.04	0.17	0.27	0.06	TF	1.00		0.03		0.50	7.00	0.23
SOYA PRODUCTS													
Soya, cheese	0.00	0.26	0.62	1.12	0.20	2.50	0.00	0.00				35.00	
Soya, milk	0.00	0.06	0.27	0.11	0.07	0.00	0.00	0.00				19.00	
Soya, milk, powder									0.74				
Soya, Miso	9.00	0.09	0.25	0.86	0.21	0.1	0.00					33.00	0.26
Soya, Natto	0.00	0.16	0.19	0.00			13.00						
Soya, Tempeh	69.00	0.13	0.11	4.60	0.29	0.84	0.00					52.00	0.36
Tofu	0.00	0.06	0.02	0.10		T	0.00	0.00					
BEANS, GRAIN AND FLOUR													
Amaranth	610.00	0.08	0.16	1.40									
Barley, light, pearled	0.00	0.12	0.05	3.10			0.00						
Barley, pot, dry	TR	0.21	0.07	3.70									
Beans, black, dry	TR	0.25	0.02	0.52			0.00						
Beans, blackeye, boiled	35.00	0.30	0.11	1.40			17.00						
Beans, blackeye, dry	1.00	0.59	0.22	7.70		0.00	1.00	0.00				439.00	

INGREDIENTS per 100g = 3.527oz	VITAMIN A RE mcg	VITAMIN B1 mg	VITAMIN B2 mg	VITAMIN B3 mg	VITAMIN B6 mg	VITAMIN B12 mcg	VITAMIN C mg	VITAMIN D mcg	VITAMIN E mg	VITAMIN K mg	BIOTIN mcg	FOLIC ACID mcg	PANTO-THENIC ACID mg
Beans, blackeye, frozen, boiled	17.00	0.40	0.11	1.40			9.00						
Beans, butter, boiled	TR					0.00	0.00	0.00					
Beans, butter, dry	TR	0.45	0.13	2.50	0.58	0.00	0.00	0.00				110.00	1.00
Beans, Great Northern, boiled	0.00	0.13	0.07	0.72			0.00						
Beans, Great Northern, dry	0.00	0.13	0.07	0.72			0.00						
Beans, haricot, boiled	TR					0.00	0.00	0.00					
Beans, haricot, dry	TR	0.45	0.13	2.50	0.56	0.00	0.00	0.00					0.70
Beans, lima, boiled	28.00	0.18	0.10	1.30			17.00						
Beans, lima, canned	126.00	0.04	0.04	0.19			7.05						
Beans, lima, dry	0.00	0.13	0.05	0.38			0.00						
Beans, mung, dry	4.00	0.45	0.20	2.00	0.50	0.00	TR	0.00				140.00	
Beans, pea/navy, boiled	0.00	0.13	0.07	0.72			0.00						
Beans, pea/navy, dry		1.40	0.06	0.38			0.00						
Beans, pinto, canned	0.00	0.10	0.06	0.29			0.70					60.20	0.14
Beans, pinto, dry	TR	0.18	0.08	0.38	0.07	0.00	0.00						
Beans, red kidney, boiled	TR	0.11	0.06	0.70			TR						
Beans, red kidney, canned	0.00	0.10	0.08	0.50	0.02		1.10					50.60	0.15
Beans, red kidney, dry	TR	0.54	0.18	2.00	0.44	0.00	TR	0.00				130.00	0.50
Beans, soya, boiled	1.80	0.10	0.06	0.29			0.00						

INGREDIENTS per 100g = 3.527oz	VITAMIN A RE mcg	VITAMIN B1 mg	VITAMIN B2 mg	VITAMIN B3 mg	VITAMIN B6 mg	VITAMIN B12 mcg	VITAMIN C mg	VITAMIN D mcg	VITAMIN E mg	VITAMIN K mg	BIOTIN mcg	FOLIC ACID mcg	PANTO-THENIC ACID mg
Beans, soya, canned	34.00	0.06					2.00						
Beans, soya, raw	4.00	1.10	0.31	2.20		0.00		0.00				100.00	
Bran, oat		0.77	0.20		0.20				3.3IU				
Bran, wheat	0.00	0.89	0.36	29.60	1.38	0.00	0.00	0.00	0.20		45.00	260.00	2.40
Bread, cracked wheat	TR	0.38	0.38	3.30			TR						
Bread, cracked wheat, toasted	TR	0.33	0.42	6.60			TR						
Bread, French/Vienna	TR	0.46	0.35	4.00			TR						
Bread, pumpernickel	0.00	0.33	0.51	3.30			0.00						
Bread, rye	0.00	0.40	0.31	3.30			0.00						
Bread, rye, toasted	0.00	0.36	0.36	3.60			0.00						
Bread, wholewheat	0.00	0.34	0.09	4.10	0.12	0.00	0.00	0.00	0.20		6.00	39.00	0.60
Bread, wholewheat, toasted	TR	0.33	0.42	3.80			TR						
Breadcrumbs	0.00	0.35	0.35	4.80			0.00	0.00					
Buckwheat		0.28	0.07	2.80	0.40	0.00	0.00	0.00	TR				1.20
Bulgur wheat, dry	0.00	0.28	0.14	4.50			0.00						
Chick pea/garbanzo, boiled	8.00	0.11	0.05	0.50		0.00	3.00	0.00				37.00	
Chick pea/garbanzo, dried	31.00	0.50	0.15	1.50	4.20	0.00	3.00	0.00				180.00	
Corn, tortillas		0.16	0.10	1.30			0.00						
Corn/maize meal	0.00	0.26	0.08	1.00				0.00					
Flour, buckwheat	0.00	0.08	0.04	0.40			0.00						
Flour, buckwheat, dark	0.00	0.58	0.15	2.80			0.00						

INGREDIENTS per 100g = 3.527 oz

INGREDIENTS	VITAMIN A RE mcg	VITAMIN B1 mg	VITAMIN B2 mg	VITAMIN B3 mg	VITAMIN B6 mg	VITAMIN B12 mcg	VITAMIN C mg	VITAMIN D mcg	VITAMIN E mg	VITAMIN K mg	BIOTIN mcg	FOLIC ACID mcg	PANTOTHENIC ACID mg
Flour, buckwheat, light	0.00	0.08	0.04	0.40			0.00	0.00					
Flour, carob	TR	0.05	0.05	1.50			TR						
Flour, corn/maize, dry	44.00	0.14	0.05	1.00			0.00						
Flour, lima bean													
Flour, rye	0.00	0.40	0.22	1.00	0.20	0.00	0.00	0.00	1.60				
Flour, soya, full fat		0.75	0.28	2.00	0.46	0.00	0.00	0.00	1.50			345.00	1.60
Flour, soya, low fat		0.90	0.29	2.40	0.52	0.00	0.00	0.00				410.00	1.80
Flour, wheat, wholemeal	0.00	0.47	0.09	5.70	0.50	0.00	0.00	0.00	1.40		7.00	57.00	0.80
Hominy/corn, grits, dry	44.00	0.44	0.26	3.50			0.00						
Lentils, boiled	3.00	0.11	0.04	0.40	0.11	0.00	TR	0.00				5.00	0.31
Lentils, raw	6.00	0.50	0.20	2.00	0.60	0.00	TR	0.00	TR			35.00	1.36
Millet, flour	0.00	0.68	0.19	1.30		0.00	0.00						
Millet, whole, dry	0.00	0.73	0.38	2.30			0.00						
Oatmeal	0.00	0.50	0.10	1.00	0.12	0.00	0.00	0.00	1.70		20.00	60.00	1.00
Oats, rolled, boiled	0.00	0.08	0.02	0.10			0.00						
Oats, rolled, dried	0.00	0.60	0.14	1.00			0.00						
Peas, dried	41.00	0.60	0.30	3.00	0.13	0.00	TR	0.00	TR			33.00	2.00
Peas, dried, boiled	13.00	1.00	0.07	1.00		0.00	TR	0.00	TR				
Peas, split, dried	25.00	0.70	0.20	3.20	0.13	0.00	TR	0.00	TR			33.00	2.00
Peas, split, dried, boiled	0.00	0.11	0.06	1.00		0.00	TR	0.00	TR				
Popcorn, popped	10.00	0.10	0.20	0.60			0.00						
Quinoa, dry							0.00						
Rice, bran	0.00	2.26	0.25	29.00			0.00						

INGREDIENTS per 100g = 3.527oz	VITAMIN A RE mcg	VITAMIN B1 mg	VITAMIN B2 mg	VITAMIN B3 mg	VITAMIN B6 mg	VITAMIN B12 mcg	VITAMIN C mg	VITAMIN D mcg	VITAMIN E mg	VITAMIN K mg	BIOTIN mcg	FOLIC ACID mcg	PANTO-THENIC ACID mg
Rice, brown, boiled	0.00	0.14	0.02	1.30		0.00	0.00		0.30			10.00	
Rice, brown, raw	0.00	0.59	0.07	5.30			0.00	0.00	0.80			49.00	
Rice, wild	0.00	0.45	0.63	6.20			0.00						
Rye, wholegrain	0.00	0.43	0.22	1.60			0.00						
Sago	0.00	TR	TR	TR	TR	0.00	0.00	0.00	TR		TR	TR	TR
Sorghum, grain	0.00	0.38	0.15	3.90			0.00						
Tapioca, dry	0.00	0.00	0.00	0.00			0.00						
Wheat, durum	0.00	0.66	0.12	4.40			0.00						TR
Wheatgerm	0.00	2.01	0.72	4.50	3.30	0.00	0.00		22.00		25.00	331.00	1.90

OILS

Almond
Apricot kernel
Cocoa butter
Coconut
Cod liver
Corn
Cottonseed
Grapeseed
Hazelnut
Linseed
Olive
Palm
Palm kernel
Peanut

INGREDIENTS
per 100g = 3.527oz

	VITAMIN A RE mcg	VITAMIN B1 mg	VITAMIN B2 mg	VITAMIN B3 mg	VITAMIN B6 mg	VITAMIN B12 mcg	VITAMIN C mg	VITAMIN D mcg	VITAMIN E mg	VITAMIN K mg	BIOTIN mcg	FOLIC ACID mcg	PANTO-THENIC ACID mg
Poppyseed													
Ricebran													
Safflower													
Sesame													
Soyabean													
Soyabean lecithin													
Sunflower													
Walnut													
Wheatgerm													
CONDIMENTS													
Arrowroot	0.00	TR	TR	TR	TR		0.00	0.00	TR		TR	TR	TR
Baking powder	0.00	TR	TR	TR	TR		0.00	0.00	TR		TR	TR	TR
Barmene	TR	1.00	2.00	40.00	2.50		6.00	0.00	0.00		TR	90.00	0.12
Dill pickle	20.00	TR	0.01	TR			6.00						
Fructose													
Ginger root, fresh	10.00	0.02	0.04	0.70			4.00						
Honey	0.00	TR	TR	0.30			1.00						
Honeycomb	0.00	TR	0.05	0.20			TR	0.00	TR				
Honey, in jar	0.00	TR	0.05	0.20			TR	0.00					
Marmite	0.00	3.10	11.00	58.00	1.30		0.00	0.00				1010.00	
Molasses, blackstrap		0.11	0.19	2.00									
Mustard, prepared		TR	0.20	TR			TR						
Salt	0.00	TR											
Tahini													

INGREDIENTS per 100g = 3.527oz	VITAMIN A RE mcg	VITAMIN B1 mg	VITAMIN B2 mg	VITAMIN B3 mg	VITAMIN B6 mg	VITAMIN B12 mcg	VITAMIN C mg	VITAMIN D mcg	VITAMIN E mg	VITAMIN K mg	BIOTIN mcg	FOLIC ACID mcg	PANTO-THENIC ACID mg
Tamari													
Vecon	83.00	5.00	6.00	50.00			100.00						0.00
Vinegar, cider apple	0.00	0.00	0.00	0.00	0.00		0.00	0.00	0.00		0.00	0.00	0.00
Vinegar, malt													
Vinegar, white wine													
HERBS													
Basil, ground	938.00	0.14	0.31	6.94			61.22						
Bay leaf, powdered	618.00	0.00	0.42	2.00			46.50					0.00	
Chervil, dried	566.00	TR	TR	TR	1.20								
Chives, fresh													
Dill weed, fresh	807.00	0.41	0.28	2.80	1.40								
Marjoram, dried	690.00	0.28	0.31	4.12			51.43						
Oregano, dried		0.34		6.20				0.00					
Parsley, dried	2334.00	0.17	1.23	7.90	1.00		122.04						
Parsley, fresh	850.00	0.11	0.26	1.16			171.00						
Rosemary, dried	313.00	0.51		1.00			61.00	0.00					
Sage, ground	590.00	0.75	0.33	5.72									
Savory, ground	513.00	0.36		4.08			32.38						
Tarragon, ground	420.00	0.25	1.33	8.95									
Thyme, ground	380.00	0.51	0.39	4.94									
NUTS													
Almond	0.00	0.23	0.92	3.50			TR						
Brazil	TR	1.00	0.10	1.70			TR	0.00					

INGREDIENTS per 100g = 3.527oz

	VITAMIN A RE mcg	VITAMIN B1 mg	VITAMIN B2 mg	VITAMIN B3 mg	VITAMIN B6 mg	VITAMIN B12 mcg	VITAMIN C mg	VITAMIN D mcg	VITAMIN E mg	VITAMIN K mg	BIOTIN mcg	FOLIC ACID mcg	PANTO-THENIC ACID mg
Cashew	0.00	0.20	0.20	1.40	0.25							9.20	1.21
Chestnut, dried		0.32	0.38	1.20									
Chestnut, raw		0.22	0.22	0.60									
Hazel/Filbert	0.00	0.40	0.22	0.90	0.55		TR	0.00	21.00			72.00	15.00
Hickory													
Macadamia	0.00	0.34	0.11	1.30			0.00						
Peanut	0.31	0.31	0.13	170.00			0.00						
Peanut butter	0.00	0.17	0.10	15.00	0.50		TR	0.00	4.70			53.00	2.10
Pecan		0.85	0.12	0.90			1.80		TR				
Pine/Piñon	3.50	1.25	0.21	4.00			3.50						
Pistachio	22.00	229.00		1.40			0.00						
Walnut, black	28.00	0.10	0.70	0.70			TR						
Walnut, English	14.00	0.39	0.10	1.00			3.00						
SEEDS													
Linseed/Linquist Gold													
Melon	TR	0.10	0.15	1.50			TR	0.00					
Poppy	TR	0.94	0.17	0.97	0.44								
Pumpkin	39.00	0.20	0.30	1.70			TR						
Safflower		1.10	0.41	2.20			0.00						
Sesame	12.50	0.75	0.13	5.00			0.00						
Sunflower	3.50	2.30	0.25	4.60			TR						
SPICES													
Allspice	54.00	0.10	0.06	2.80			39.20	0.00					

INGREDIENTS per 100g = 3.527oz	VITAMIN A RE mcg	VITAMIN B1 mg	VITAMIN B2 mg	VITAMIN B3 mg	VITAMIN B6 mg	VITAMIN B12 mcg	VITAMIN C mg	VITAMIN D mcg	VITAMIN E mg	VITAMIN K mg	BIOTIN mcg	FOLIC ACID mcg	PANTO-THENIC ACID mg
Aniseed													
Asafoetida	0.60	0.00	0.04	0.30			0.00	0.00					
Caraway	36.00	0.38	0.37	3.60				0.00					
Cardamom pod, ground	TR	0.19	0.18	1.10			0.19	0.00					
Celery	TR	0.50	0.50	5.00			TR						
Chili, powder	3493.00	0.34	0.79	7.89			64.14	0.00					
Cinnamon	43.00	TR	TR	TR			43.00						
Cloves, ground	53.00	0.11	0.26	1.45			80.81						
Coriander, leaves, dried	TR	1.25	1.50	10.70			567.00						
Coriander, seed		0.23	0.29	2.10				0.00					
Cumin, seed	127.00	0.62	0.32	4.57			7.71	0.00					
Curry leaves, raw	1000.00	0.08	0.21	2.30			12.00	0.00					
Curry powder	99.00	0.25	0.28	3.40			11.40	0.00					
Dill, seed	5.00	0.41	0.28	2.80				0.00					
Fennel, seed	14.00	0.40	0.35	6.00			3.00	0.00	0.00				
Fenugreek, seed		0.32	0.36	1.64								57.00	
Garlic, powder		0.35	TR	TR			TR						
Ginger, ground	15.00	0.04	0.18	5.15									
Mustard, powder	0.00						0.00	0.00					
Mustard, seed	6.00	0.54	0.38	7.80									
Nutmeg, powder	10.00	0.34	0.05	1.20				0.00					
Onion, powder		4.70	TR	TR			TR						
Paprika	6060.00	0.65	1.74	15.32			71.00	0.00					

INGREDIENTS per 100g = 3.527oz	VITAMIN A RE mcg	VITAMIN B1 mg	VITAMIN B2 mg	VITAMIN B3 mg	VITAMIN B6 mg	VITAMIN B12 mcg	VITAMIN C mg	VITAMIN D mcg	VITAMIN E mg	VITAMIN K mg	BIOTIN mcg	FOLIC ACID mcg	PANTO-THENIC ACID mg
Pepper, black	TR	TR	0.47	TR			0.00						
Pepper, cayenne	4161.00	0.32	0.91	8.70			76.44						
Pepper, white	TR	0.02	0.12	0.21									
Saffron													
Turmeric	TR	0.15	0.23	5.10			26.00	0.00					
Yeast, bakers, dried	TR	15.60	4.25	37.50			TR	0.00					
Yeast, brewers	TR	15.00	4.25	37.50			TR						
Yeast, brewers debittered	TR	15.60	4.28	37.90									
Yeast, torula	TR	14.01	5.06	44.40									

3. Doses and toxic levels of nutrients

This is a quick reference list of doses and toxic level intakes for adults. For more details of intakes for children and old people I recommend *The Good Nutrients Guide*† by Rita Greer and Robert Woodward, details of which are on page 131. An explanation of the different modes in which some nutrient values are expressed, both on various products and in various publications, is given at the end of this section.

Nutrient	RDA	Dosage/Toxicity
Vitamin A Retinol	750–1000 mcg	Not more than 2000 mcg daily
Vitamin B1 Thiamin	1–1.5 mg	5 mg considered enough for most people. No known toxicity up to 500 mg
Vitamin B2 Riboflavin	1.3–1.8 mg	5 mg considered safe. No known toxic levels
Vitamin B3 Niacin or Nicotinic acid	15–20 mg	If in the form of nicotinamide up to 100 mg
Vitamin B5 Pantothenic acid	4–7 mg	Dose in excess of 2 g per day may cause diarrhoea in some people. No other problems even in doses up to 25 g

Vitamin B6 Pyridoxine	2–2.2 mg	Supplements up to 100 mg. Overdose 500 mg
Vitamin B12 Cyanocobalamin	3 mcg	Supplements usually up to 5–50 mcg. No known toxic levels
Vitamin B15 Pangamic acid	No RDA	No known toxicity with doses up to 50 mg
Folic acid	400 mcg	No known toxicity with doses up to 50 mg. No known toxicity up to 15 mg daily but certain blood tests used for diagnostic purposes are affected, and if you are taking Folic Acid in supplement form tell your doctor if you have tests
PABA (Para amino benzoic acid)	No RDA	Doses between 10 and 100 mg have no known toxicity
Choline	No RDA	Doses between 10 and 1000 mg have no known toxicity
Inositol	No RDA	See reference book[†]
Vitamin C Ascorbic acid	50–60 mg	3 g considered to be the safe level unless under supervision
Vitamin D (sunshine vitamin)	200–400 iu	None up to 2000 iu
Vitamin E D-alphato-copherol	No RDA	10 iu used in supplements
Vitamin H Biotin	100–300 mcg	No known toxicity levels
Vitamin K	100–250 mcg	Up to 500 mcg considered safe

Vitamin P Bioflavinoid	No RDA	Up to 1/10th as much as the dose of vitamin C. No toxic level known
Boron		3 mg sometimes used. The toxic level is unknown but products should be prepared from organic boron sources
Calcium	500 mg	Some nutritionists recommend up to 2000 mg of elemental calcium
Chlorine (as chloride)	4–5 mg	See reference book[†]
Chromium	200 mcg	See reference book[†]
Copper	2–3 mg	If taken as elemental copper. 10 mg if taken as dried copper sulphate
Iodine	150–200 mcg	As free iodine. From true organic sources such as kelp 500 mcg is not excessive
Iron	10–15 mg	If in ferrous form 15–20 mg
Magnesium	200–500 mg	20 g is considered toxic
Manganese	2–3 mg	Up to 20 mg considered safe
Molybdenum	100 mcg	Or 2 mcg per kilo body weight. Not more than 100 mcg recommended
Phosphorus	800–1200 mg	No known toxicity levels
Potassium	4000 mg	No known toxicity levels, but supplements should be from potassium orotate or potassium

		chloride. Potassium gluconate not recommended in tablet form but may be taken as a powder
Selenium	150–200 mcg	Up to 200 mcg considered safe in supplement form as organic selenium
Silicon	No RDA	The most abundant element on earth. Nearly all passes straight through the body
Sodium	2000–3500 mg	If processed foods are eaten then no supplements are necessary
Sulphur	No RDA	No toxicity known from dietary sulphur
Zinc	2–3 mg	Up to 20 mg to 100 mg elemental zinc in divided doses is considered safe

†The Good Nutrients Guide *by Rita Greer and Dr Robert Woodward, available from The Cantassium Co., 225 Putney Bridge Road, London SW15.*

4. Conversion factors of nutrient values

Vitamin A
Derived from animals, mcg vitamin A is expressed as mcg retinol. Derived from plants, mcg vitamin A is expressed as mcg carotene.

Sometimes one sees retinol and carotene expressed by the earlier symbols; 'iu' (international units). However, the modern practice is to refer to mcg vitamin A as mcg RE (retinol equivalents), being a calculation that includes both mcg retinol and mcg carotene:

- To convert 1 mcg carotene into 1 mcg RE: divide the carotene by 6.
- To convert 1 iu carotene into 1 mcg RE: divide the carotene by 10.
- To convert 1 iu retinol into 1 mcg RE: divide retinol by 3.33.
- 1 mcg retinol = 1 mcg RE.

Carotene is water soluble, while retinol is fat soluble. Carotene is not so readily converted to vitamin A by the body; it also absorbs oxygen easily and therefore loses its potency.

Vitamin B3
Nicotinic acid, niacin or niacinamide are the names given to this vitamin. When these names are followed by 'equivalent', this means that there is an additional estimated amount of vitamin B3 that the body will have made from eating foods that contain the amino acid tryptophan (in protein).

B vitamins
It is important to remember that all B vitamins should be taken together, as an excess of one will cause a deficiency in others.

5. Major vitamins and minerals individually rated

This is a quick reference list of a selection of foods containing specific vitamins and minerals rated by their value, in either microgrammes (mcg), or milligrammes (mg). The foods with high values are at the tops of the lists.

Calcium in mg per 100 grammes of food (3.527 oz)

Whitebait fried	860	Tripe stewed	150
Leaf concentrate*	829	Dandelion leaves	
Cheddar cheese	720	boiled	140
Spinach boiled	600	Pistachio nuts	140
Sardines canned in oil	550	Spring onions	140
Brie cheese	540	Eggs raw	130
Tofu	507	Milk skimmed	120
Soya cheese	450	Beetroot tops	119
Seaweed, nori/kelp		Milk whole	115
soaked	357	Beetroot tops cooked	113
Parsley	330	Broccoli florets raw	100
Dried figs	280	Goats' milk	100
Almonds, no shell	250	Bok choy cooked	93
Watercress	220	Tempeh	93
Mussels boiled	200	Broccoli boiled	76
Pink salmon canned	196	Savoy cabbage raw	76
Goats' milk cheese	190	Kale boiled	72
Turnip greens raw	190	Seaweed kelp/kombu	
Oysters raw	190	raw	68
Brazil nuts	178	Soya beans cooked	68
Sheeps' milk	170	Miso	66

Kipper baked	65	Wheatmeal flour	38
Chick peas boiled	64	Alfalfa sprouts raw	33
Leeks boiled	63	Herring grilled	33
Blackcurrants raw	60	Crab boiled	29
Oatmeal	55	Red kidney beans	
Celery raw	52	canned	24
French beans boiled	39	Coley steamed	19

Zinc in mg per 100 grammes of food (3.527 oz)

Oysters raw	45	Wholemeal bread	1.80
Wheatgerm	17	Rocquefort cheese	1.60
Wheatbran	16.20	Eggs	1.30
Whelks boiled	7.20	Butter beans cooked	1.00
Beef brisket boiled	6.30	Peas boiled	1.00
Winkles boiled	5.70	Parsley	0.90
Crab boiled	5.50	Peas raw	0.70
Shrimps boiled	5.30	Brown rice cooked	0.70
Beef rumpsteak		Goats' milk cheese	
grilled	5.30	soft	0.70
Lamb leg roast	5.30	Sheeps' milk	0.70
Parmesan cheese	5.30	Cottage cheese plain	0.60
Beef topside roast	4.90	Broccoli florets, raw	0.60
Leaf concentrate*	4.10	Goats' milk	0.50
Bacon collar boiled	3.90	Brussels sprouts raw	0.50
Soya flour full-fat	3.90	Figs dried stewed	0.50
Miso	3.32	Carrots old	0.40
Gammon rasher		Spinach boiled	0.40
grilled	3.20	Tomatoes canned	0.30
Oatmeal	3.00	Cauliflower raw	0.30
Wholemeal flour	2.90	Carrots boiled	0.30
Pork chop grilled	2.90	Asparagus boiled	0.30
Ham	2.30	Figs fresh	0.30
Cheddar cheese	2.30	Guava	0.20
Tempeh	1.81	Tomatoes raw	0.20
Gouda cheese	1.80	Peppers raw	0.20
Soya cheese	1.80		

Iron in mg per 100 grammes of food (3.527 oz)

Cockles boiled	26	Pistachio nuts	14
Winkles boiled	15	Linquist Gold	12

Wheatgerm	8.5	Borage raw	3.3
Parsley	8.0	Pumpkin leaves	
Melon seed	8.0	cooked	3.2
Sesame seeds	7.5	Dandelion leaves raw	3.1
Calf's liver	7.3	Beef bottom round	
Beef regular ground	7.0	cooked	3.0
Sunflower seeds	6.7	Piñon/pine nuts	3.0
Oysters raw	6.6	Scallops steamed	3.0
Seaweed kelp/kombu		Wheatbran	2.9
soaked	6.1	Beef canned corned	
Cashew nuts	6.0	UK style	2.9
Lambs sweetbread		Beef brisket boiled	2.8
raw	5.6	Endive raw	2.8
Peas dried	4.7	Miso	2.74
Sardines canned in		Peaches dried stewed	2.5
tomato	4.6	Persimmons raw	2.5
Oatbran	4.5	Prunes dried	2.4
Dried figs	4.3	Courgette/zucchini	2.4
Beef canned corned		Vine leaves	2.3
US style	4.3	Tempeh	2.2
Oatmeal	4.1	Mangetout cooked	2.0
Dried apricots	4.1	Mulberries raw	1.85
Wholemeal flour	3.9	Shrimps boiled	1.8
Desiccated coconut	3.6	Butter beans cooked	1.7
Jerusalem artichokes		Elderberries raw	1.6
raw	3.4	Tofu	1.2
Rump steak grilled	3.4	Raspberries raw	1.2
Beetroot tops raw	3.3	Whitecurrants cooked	0.8

Folic acid in mcg per 100 grammes of food (3.527 oz)

Chicken liver fried	500	Spring greens boiled	110
Soya flour full-fat	345	Butter beans dry	110
Wheatgerm	331	Peanuts	110
Endive raw	330	Camembert cheese	102
Calf's liver fried	320	Marrow boiled	97
Ox liver stewed	290	Almonds	96
Wheatbran	260	Cucumber	96
Turnip greens raw	194	French beans boiled	95.5
Chick peas dried	180	Curly endive	94
Spinach cooked	140	Kale boiled	91
Broccoli cooked	110	Alfalfa sprouts	91

Leeks boiled	90.8	Spring onions	40
Cabbage winter raw	90	Asparagus boiled	30
Cabbage savoy boiled	90	Melon cantaloupe raw	30
Cabbage red raw	90	Salmon steamed	29
Beetroot raw	90	French beans boiled	28
Brussels sprouts raw	88	Runner beans boiled	28
Brussels sprouts		White cabbage raw	26
boiled	87	Dates dried	21
Avocado pear	66	Soya milk	19
Runner beans raw	60	Blackcurrants dried	11
Oatmeal	60	Brown rice cooked	10
Wholemeal flour	57	Spaghetti squash	
Eggs	51	cooked	8
Red kidney beans		Cows' milk whole	6
canned	50	Lentils boiled	5
Beetroot cooked	50		

Potassium in mg per 100 grammes of food (3.527 oz)

Figs dried	1010	Bloater grilled/broiled	450
Seaweed kelp/kombu	978	Jerusalem artichokes	
Wheatgerm	950	boiled	420
Beetroot tops	900	Sesame seeds	412
Almonds	860	Butter beans cooked	400
Raisins	860	Celeriac boiled	400
Sultanas	860	Chick peas boiled	400
Pumpkin seeds	817	Cardoon raw	400
Dates dried	750	Shrimps boiled	400
Peanut butter	700	Pecans	391
Sunflower seeds	695	Winter cabbage	390
Brazil nuts	607	Bean sprouts raw	380
Cress	606	Lamb cutlets grilled	380
Cashew nuts	565	Pork chops grilled	380
Potatoes baked in		Bok choy cooked	371
skin	550	Herrings grilled	370
Halibut grilled/broiled	518	Blackcurrants raw	370
Walnuts	507	Tempeh	367
Chestnuts	500	Banana	350
Purslane raw	494	Coley steamed	350
Spinach boiled	490	Trout	349
Borage	470	Kohlrabi boiled	340
Mushrooms raw	470	Broccoli florets	340

Prunes stewed	334	Okra pods cooked	322
Kiwi fruit peeled	332	Melon cantaloupe	320

Riboflavin in mg per 100 grammes of food (3.527 oz)

Calf's liver fried	4.2	Salsify cooked	0.17
Lamb's kidney fried	2.3	Crab boiled	0.15
Dried egg	1.8	New Zealand spinach,	
Rocquefort cheese	0.65	raw	0.13
Goats' milk cheese		Purslane raw	0.11
soft	0.63	Tuna canned in oil	0.11
Soya cheese	0.63	Tuna canned in water	0.10
Eggs	0.47	Prunes stewed	0.10
Cheddar cheese	0.40	Sultanas/golden	
Eel stewed	0.40	raisins	0.08
Rump steak grilled	0.36	Figs dried	0.08
Edam cheese	0.35	Sweetcorn boiled	0.08
Sheeps' milk	0.32	Seaweed kelp/kombu	0.08
Broccoli florets raw	0.30	Cod fillet raw	0.07
Beetroot tops cooked	0.29	Cherries eating	0.07
Soya milk	0.27	Banana	0.07
Vine leaves	0.24	Blackcurrants raw	0.06
Forerib beef roast	0.24	Elderberries raw	0.06
Lamb's brains boiled	0.24	Redcurrants raw	0.05
Coley raw	0.20	Figs fresh	0.05
Broccoli boiled	0.20	Blackberries raw	0.04
Apricots dried	0.20	Apricots cooked	0.04
Milk skimmed		Greengages	0.03
pasteurized	0.18	Bilberries	0.02
Herring grilled	0.18	Grapefruit flesh	0.02
Dandelion leaves raw	0.17	Apples cooking	0.02

Vitamin A retinol equivalents (RE) in mcg per 100 grammes of food (3.527 oz)

Lamb's liver fried	20610	Dandelion leaves raw	1400
Ox liver stewed	20350	Dandelion leaves	
Chicken liver fried	11116	boiled	1170
Leaf concentrate*	6500	Cress	930
Carrots boiled	2000	Butter	886
Carrots old raw	2000	Parsley	850
Sweet potatoes baked	1727	Kale boiled	740

Spring greens boiled	666	Endive raw	333
Beetroot tops raw	610	Cheese goats' milk	
Spinach boiled	600	soft	310
Turnip greens cooked	550	Lettuce romaine/cos	189
Beetroot tops cooked	509	Lettuce round	166
Watercress	500	Purslane raw	133
New Zealand spinach		Pumpkin cooked	108
raw	440	Tomato raw	100
Cream cheese	421	Sheeps' milk	83
Borage raw	420	Goats' milk	44
Broccoli boiled	416	Plums raw	36
Cheshire Cheese	386	Green pepper raw	36
Cream single	347		

Vitamin C in mg per 100 grammes of food (3.527 oz)

Parsley	150	Broccoli boiled	34
Broccoli florets raw	110	Broad beans raw	33
Green pepper raw	100	Orange juice fresh	32
Kiwi fruit peeled	98	Swiss chard raw	30
Brussels sprouts raw	90	Beetroot tops	30
Persimmon raw	66	New Zealand spinach	
Papaya	61	raw	30
Savoy cabbage raw	60	Lime juice fresh	29
Cauliflower florets		Raspberries	25
raw	60	Mustard greens	
Strawberries	60	boiled	25
Watercress	60	Broccoli tops cooked	25
Turnip greens raw	60	Asparagus boiled	20
Mangetout raw	60	New Zealand spinach	
Cabbage red raw	55	cooked	16
Lemon juice fresh	50	Courgette/zucchini	
Mooli	42	raw	16
Cabbage white raw	40	Avocado	15
Lychees raw	40	Beansprouts, mung	13
Kale boiled	40	Bok choy cooked	12
Mustard and cress	40	Purslane cooked	10
Brussels sprouts		Celery boiled	10
boiled	40	Alfalfa sprouts	9
Loganberries	35	Celeriac raw	8
Dandelion leaves	35	Salsify raw	8
Borage raw	35	Cucumber	8

Celery raw	7	Carrots old raw	6
Beetroot cooked	6	Celeriac boiled	4

Thiamin Vitamin B1 in mg per 100 grammes of food (3.527 oz)

Pumpkin seeds	39.00	Sweetcorn boiled	0.15
Walnuts	28.00	Parsley	0.15
Almonds shelled	14.00	Brown rice cooked	0.14
Sesame seeds	12.50	Tempeh	0.13
Sunflower seeds	3.50	Lentils boiled	0.11
Piñons/pine nuts	3.50	Chick peas boiled	0.11
Seaweed, spirulina	3.00	Coley raw	0.10
Wheatgerm	2.00	New potatoes boiled	0.10
Peas dried boiled	1.00	Asparagus	0.10
Dandelion leaves raw	0.90	Broad beans boiled	0.10
Wheatbran	0.89	Beetroot tops cooked	0.10
Oatbran	0.77	Watercress	0.10
Sweet potatoes baked in skin	0.70	Dried figs	0.10
Lamb's liver fried	0.56	Raisins	0.10
Dried prunes	0.53	Leeks raw	0.10
Oatmeal	0.50	Mushrooms raw	0.10
Wholemeal flour	0.47	Red kidney beans canned	0.10
Rye flour	0.40	Kumquats raw	0.08
Turnip greens cooked	0.40	Buckwheat flour	0.08
Peas raw	0.32	Rump steak grilled	0.08
Figs fresh	0.30	Orange flesh	0.08
Peas boiled	0.25	Tofu	0.06
Guava	0.25	Banana	0.04
Leaf concentrate*	0.20	Purslane raw	0.03
Apricots dried	0.20	Seaweed kelp/kombu soaked	0.03
Apples dried	0.20		
Salmon raw	0.20		

Niacin Vitamin B3 in mg per 100 grammes of food (3.527 oz)

Calf's liver fried	15.6	Tuna fish canned in oil	12.9
Lamb's liver fried	15.2	Seaweed, spirulina dried	12.8
Tuna fish canned in water	15.0		

Leaf concentrate*	10.9	Beansprouts, mung raw	0.7
Turkey breast	10.0	Goats' milk cheese	
Halibut grilled/broiled	9.0	soft	0.65
Mackerel fried	8.7	Aubergine/eggplant	
Rabbit stewed	8.5	cooked	0.6
Chicken roasted	8.2	Cauliflower florets	
Pilchard canned in		raw	0.6
tomatoes	7.6	Leeks raw	0.6
Turkey dark meat	6.7	Kale boiled	0.5
Red salmon baked	5.5	Celeriac boiled	0.5
Halibut steamed	5.2	Runner beans boiled	0.5
Haddock fillet		Stilton cheese	0.49
steamed	5.1	Purslane raw	0.48
Mushrooms raw	4.0	Sheeps' milk	0.41
Lemon sole cooked	3.6	Brussels sprouts	
Broad beans boiled	3.0	boiled	0.40
Eel stewed	2.8	Carrots boiled	0.40
Peas raw	2.5	Goats' milk	0.31
Seaweed kelp/kombu	2.1	Red cabbage raw	0.30
Broad beans raw	1.5	White cabbage raw	0.30
Jerusalem artichokes		Bok choy cooked	0.17
raw	1.3	Whole milk	0.09
Soya cheese	1.2	Cheddar cheese	0.07
Broccoli florets	1.0	Vine leaves	0.05
Beetroot tops	0.9	Butter	0.01
Asparagus boiled	0.8		

Pyridoxine Vitamin B6 in mg per 100 grammes of food (3.527 oz)

Wheatgerm	3.30	Brussels sprouts raw	0.28
Wheatbran	1.38	Turnip greens raw	0.26
Mackerel fried	0.84	Prunes dried	0.26
Salmon raw	0.75	Leeks raw	0.25
Smoked haddock fillet		Cress	0.24
steamed	0.35	Elderberries	0.23
Rump steak		Red cabbage raw	0.21
grilled/broiled	0.33	Miso	0.21
Currants	0.30	Broccoli florets raw	0.21
Sultanas/golden		Parsley	0.20
raisins	0.30	Oatbran	0.20
Tempeh	0.29	New potatoes boiled	0.20

Cauliflower florets	0.20	Potatoes baked in	
Sweetcorn on cob	0.19	skin	0.14
Spinach boiled	0.18	Watercress	0.13
Old potatoes boiled	0.18	Cauliflower boiled	0.12
Celeriac raw	0.17	Lentils boiled	0.11
Green pepper raw	0.17	Spaghetti squash	
Spring greens boiled	0.16	cooked	0.10
Savoy cabbage boiled	0.16	Radishes	0.10
White cabbage raw	0.16	Lettuce round	0.07
Leeks boiled	0.15	Bilberries raw	0.06

*Information on leaf concentrate can be obtained from Find Your Feet, 318 St Pauls Road, London N1 2LF, England. (Phone: 071-354 4430).

6. Elements required by the body and alternative names of some nutrients

- Oxygen
- Water
- Carbohydrate
- Fat
- Protein

Vitamins

Fat Soluble Vitamins
- Vitamin A retinol, retinol equivalents, carotene(s)
- Vitamin D sunshine vitamin
- Vitamin E d-alphatocopherol
- Vitamin K

Water Soluble Vitamins
- Vitamin B complex:
    B1 thiamin
    B2 riboflavin
    B3 nicotinic acid, niacin, niacinamide
    B5 pantothenic acid, pantothenate or calcium pantothenate
    B6 pyridoxine
    B12 cyanocobalamin
    Biotin
    Choline
    Folic acid, folacin, folate inositol
    PABA (Para amino benzoic acid)
- B15 pangamic acid
- Vitamin C ascorbic acid
- Vitamin P bioflavonoids

Minerals

- Boron
- Calcium
- Chlorine
- Chromium
- Copper
- Iodine
- Iron
- Magnesium
- Manganese
- Molybdenum
- Phosphorus
- Potassium
- Selenium
- Silicon
- Sodium
- Sulphur
- Vanadium
- Zinc

Many of these minerals are required by the body in minute quantities, these are known as micro-nutrients.

It is the interaction of multiple nutrients that determines their capacity for absorption and utilisation by the body.

Dr Michael Colgan Ph.D., in *Your Personal Vitamin Profile* (Published in UK by Blond and Briggs).

7. Recommended daily nutrient intake in the United Kingdom and the United States

UK recommended daily intake of calories and nutrients

	Years	Energy kcal	Protein g	Calcium mg	Iron mg	Vit A RE
Boys	up to 1	780	19	600	6	450
	1	1200	30	600	7	300
	2	1400	35	600	7	300
	3–4	1560	39	600	8	300
	5–6	1740	43	600	10	300
	7–8	1980	49	600	10	400
	9–11	2280	56	700	12	575
	12–14	2640	66	700	12	725
	15–17	2880	72	600	12	750
Girls	up to 1	720	18	600	6	450
	1	1100	27	600	7	300
	2	1300	32	600	7	300
	3–4	1500	37	600	8	300
	5–6	1680	42	600	10	300
	7–8	1900	48	600	10	400
	9–11	2050	51	700	12	575
	12–14	2150	53	600	12	725
	15–17	2150	53	600	12	750
Male 18–34	Sedentary	2510	62	500	10	750
	Moderately active	2900	72	500	10	750
	Very active	3350	84	500	10	750

	Years	Energy kcal	Protein g	Calcium mg	Iron mg	Vit A RE
35–64	Sedentary	2400	60	500	10	750
	Moderately active	2750	69	500	10	750
	Very active	3350	84	500	10	750
65–74		2400	60	500	10	750
75 and over		2150	54	500	10	750
Female						
18–54	Most occupations	2150	54	500	12	750
	Very active	2500	62	500	12	750
55–74		1900	47	500	10	750
75 and over		1680	42	500	10	750
Pregnant		2400	60	1200	13	750
Lactating		2750	69	1200	15	1200

	Years	Thiamin mg	Riboflavin mg	Niacin mg	Vit C mg	Vit D mcg
Boys	up to 1	0.3	0.4	5	20	7.5
	1	0.5	0.6	7	20	10
	2	0.6	0.7	8	20	10
	3–4	0.6	0.8	9	20	10
	5–6	0.7	0.9	10	20	
	7–8	0.8	1.0	11	20	
	9–11	0.9	1.2	14	25	
	12–14	1.1	1.4	16	25	
	15–17	1.2	1.7	19	30	
Girls	up to 1	0.3	0.4	5	20	7.5
	1	0.4	0.6	7	20	10
	2	0.5	0.7	8	20	10
	3–4	0.6	0.8	9	20	10
	5–6	0.7	0.9	10	20	
	7–8	0.8	1.0	11	20	
	9–11	0.8	1.2	14	25	
	12–14	0.9	1.4	16	25	
	15–17	0.9	1.7	19	30	
Male						
18–34	Sedentary	1.0	1.6	18	30	

	Years	Thia-min mg	Ribo-flavin mg	Niacin mg	Vit C mg	Vit D mcg
	Moderately active	1.2	1.6	18	30	
	Very active	1.3	1.6	18	30	
35–64	Sedentary	1.0	1.6	18	30	
	Moderately active	1.1	1.6	18	30	
	Very active	1.3	1.6	18	30	
65–74		1.0	1.6	18	30	
75 and over		0.9	1.6	18	30	
Female						
18–54	Most occupations	0.9	1.3	15	30	
	Very active	1.0	1.3	15	30	
55–74		0.8	1.3	15	30	
75 and over		0.7	1.3	15	30	
Pregnant		1.0	1.6	18	60	10
Lactating		1.1	1.8	21	60	10

USA recommended daily intake of calories and nutrients

	Years	Energy kcal	Protein g	Vit A RE	Vit D mg	Vit E mg
Infants	0–6 months	115*	2.2*	420	10	3
	6 months–1 year	105*	2.0*	400	10	4
Children	1–3	1300	23	400	10	5
	4–6	1700	30	500	10	6
	7–10	2400	34	700	10	7
Males	11–14	2700	45	1000	10	8
	15–18	2800	56	1000	10	10
	19–22	2900	56	1000	7.5	10
	23–50	2700	56	1000	5	10
	51+	2400	56	1000	5	10
Females	11–14	2200	46	800	10	8
	15–18	2100	46	800	10	8
	19–22	2100	44	800	7.5	8

*For each kilogramme of body weight this RDI applies

	Years	Energy kcal	Protein g	Vit A RE	Vit D mg	Vit E mg
	23–50	2000	44	800	5	8
	51+	1800	44	800	5	8
Pregnant		+300	+30	+200	+5	+2
Lactating		+500	+20	+400	+5	+3

	Years	Vit C mg	Thiamin mg	Ribo-flavin mg	Niacin mg equ
Infants	0–6 months	35	0.3	0.4	6
	6 months–1 year	35	0.5	0.6	8
Children	1–3	45	0.7	0.8	9
	4–6	45	0.9	1.0	11
	7–10	45	1.2	1.4	16
Males	11–14	50	1.4	1.6	18
	15–18	60	1.4	1.7	18
	19–22	60	1.5	1.7	19
	23–50	60	1.4	1.6	18
	51+	60	1.2	1.4	16
Females	11–14	50	1.1	1.3	15
	15–18	60	1.1	1.3	14
	19–22	60	1.1	1.3	14
	23–50	60	1.0	1.2	13
	51+	60	1.0	1.2	13
Pregnant		+20	+0.4	+0.3	+2
Lactating		+40	+0.5	+0.5	+5

	Years	Vit B6 mg	Folacin mcg	Vit B12 mcg	Calcium mg
Infants	0–6 months	0.3	30	0.5	360
	6 months–1 year	0.6	45	1.5	540
Children	1–3	0.9	100	2.0	800
	4–6	1.3	200	2.5	800
	7–10	1.6	300	3.0	800
Males	11–14	1.8	400	3.0	1200
	15–18	2.0	400	3.0	1200
	19–22	2.2	400	3.0	800
	23–50	2.2	400	3.0	800

	Years	Vit B6 mg	Folacin mcg	Vit B12 mcg	Calcium mg
	51+	2.2	400	3.0	800
Females	11–14	1.8	400	3.0	1200
	15–18	2.0	400	3.0	1200
	19–22	2.0	400	3.0	800
	23–50	2.0	400	3.0	800
	51+	2.0	400	3.0	800
Pregnant		+0.6	+400	+1.0	+400
Lactating		+0.5	+100	+1.0	+400

	Years	Phosphorus mg	Magnesium mg	Iron mg	Zinc mg	Iodine mg
Infants	0–6 months	240	50	15	10	70
	6 months–1 year	360	70	15	5	50
Children	1–3	800	150	15	10	70
	4–6	800	200	10	10	90
	7–10	800	250	10	10	120
Males	11–14	1200	350	18	15	150
	15–18	1200	400	18	15	150
	19–22	800	350	10	15	150
	23–50	800	350	10	15	150
	51+	800	350	10	15	150
Females	11–14	1200	300	18	15	150
	15–18	1200	300	18	15	150
	19–22	800	300	18	15	150
	23–50	800	300	18	15	150
	51+	800	300	10	15	150
Pregnant		+400	+150	a	+5	+25
Lactating		+400	+150	a	+10	+50

a = supplemental iron is recommended

8. How plants obtain their nutrients and energy

Before we discuss the buying, storing and cooking of food, it will be helpful if we understand the reasons for taking special care of perishable items, particularly green vegetables and soft fruits, from the moment they are picked until they are eaten.

When plants reach maturity they are picked for food, but during the growing period the plants use enzymes together with oxygen, to manufacture vitamins. The oxygen and enzymes, which helped to build the food value originally, continue to work after the plant reaches maturity to bring about the destruction of these vitamins. The aim therefore is to eat the plants when they are fully developed (preferably raw), and to do this we must inhibit further enzyme action. This can be achieved by refrigeration. When produce is left for unnecessarily long periods at room temperature, enzyme activity increases and this results in the destruction of vitamins. The activity of these oxygen-containing enzymes slows down when temperatures increase during cooking, until at boiling point they are destroyed. Washing and prolonged soaking will also leach out the nutrients.

Cutting or tearing the leaves speeds up the enzyme action, as a greater area of the plant is exposed to oxygen, resulting in further vitamin loss. Some enzymes are more active in the light, therefore it is best to store vegetables and soft fruits in a cool, dark place, such as the bottom drawer of a refrigerator. The thick skins on some fruits protect them from oxygenation.

Natural sugars in vegetables and fruits will dissolve quickly, just as table sugar does when it is added to liquid; this means that slow washing or soaking of these foods will result in sugar loss. Vegetables contain less sugar than fruits, and when the sugar is lost through soaking the flavour is quickly impaired. Washing and prolonged soaking also cause loss of aromatic oils, vitamins and minerals.

Vitamins are manufactured by the plants, and are therefore of organic origin. Minerals, however, are absorbed from the soil and are inorganic substances. An important food, full of the sun's vital energy, is chlorophyll. When a plant is subjected to the sun's rays it manufactures this substance, which is the green pigment in foliage; chlorophyll also enables photosynthesis to take place - the process by which, in the presence of sunlight, the leaves absorb carbon dioxide from the air, and water from the soil and air-borne moisture. Photosynthesis manufactures carbohydrate, which then provides us with energy from our food. During this process oxygen is given off into the atmosphere. When humans and animals eat foods containing carbohydrates, and inhale air, energy is produced. This results in carbon dioxide being given off, which, in turn, is utilized by plants and trees. Chlorophyll is a good cleanser and detoxifier for the human system. Most of it is contained in the dark outer leaves of plants, the kind that most of us throw away. Dr Bernard Jensen in his book *Vibrant Health from Your Kitchen* says 'The chemical structure of chlorophyll is almost exactly the same as the haemoglobin in red blood cells which carry vital oxygen to the tissues.' Good examples of such foods are sprouts, watercress, beetroot tops, dandelion leaves, bok choy, broccoli, kale, cabbage, turnip greens, parsley, and spinach. The richest form is an algae known as 'chlorella'.

Nutrients – their purpose
The purpose of nutrients is to provide the body with heat, energy-producing material for the growth and repair of the body tissues, and to assist in the regulation of all bodily functions. All nutrients must be present in the diet, although individuals vary in their requirements.

9. Buying, storing, preparing and cooking food to conserve nutrients

Buying food

Avoid buying fresh fruit and vegetables from shops that have heated strip-lighting immediately over the display shelf; the heat hastens the enzyme action, causing loss of vitamins and making produce wilt before you even get it home! Buy only what you need to use immediately so as to avoid prolonged storage.

In some health food shops the ambient temperature is harmful to the organic produce which is often arranged in boxes on the floor. Supermarkets, although air-conditioned, unlike health food shops, still tend to display produce on shelves which have heated strip-lighting immediately above.

For those eating meat, it is better to buy from sources where the animals have been raised under free-range conditions, and particularly where they have been fed on foods natural to their species. Intensively-reared stock usually means that the animals are fed on an unnatural diet (such as cattle fed on sheep and other offal) and are deprived of the benefits of the sunshine, air, and freedom to which they would normally be accustomed in a natural environment. Traditionally, the vegetable matter on which these animals feed is returned to the pasture in the form of manure, thus fertilizing the ground to produce more abundant crops and pasture.

Storage of food

Always buy the freshest vegetables and soft fruit you can find and, if they need to be stored, keep them in the vegetable drawer at the bottom of the refrigerator. Fruits with thick skins will keep better.

Preparation of food

When washing vegetables that have been polluted by sprays, it is recommended by Dr Alec Forbes in his book *Bristol Detox Diet* that foods should be washed rapidly in a fairly strong water-and-vinegar solution, as the acid solution removes some of the poisons. (The cheapest malt vinegar is recommended as it is the most acid.) It is suggested that the vegetables then be rinsed in clean water before eating.

After washing, the produce should be thoroughly dried; but do not forget that there are higher concentrations of vitamins and minerals in the dark outside leaves than are to be found in the paler inner ones.

A good way of preventing loss of nutrients when the leaves have been cut or torn, grated or shredded, is to toss them in olive or other salad oil to prevent oxygen in the air coming into contact with the torn surfaces, and then returning them immediately to the refrigerator. Before serving, the remainder of the dressing ingredients may be added.

The dried fruits available on the market, unless organically grown, will have been treated with sulphur as a preservative, and may also have been coated with glycerin. Pour boiling water over them and let them stand for a minute. In the case of organic fruits this procedure will also kill off any insect eggs. (Insects seem to be attracted to natural foods on which to lay their eggs to provide the grubs with nutritious foods.) In the case of artificially coated fruits, boiling water will help to dislodge these unwelcome additives, and, if these fruits are to be used for baking, allow a little less water in the recipe. Dried fruits eaten raw should always be soaked first to reconstitute them. This prevents one from eating too many, as they are high in calories due to the amount of natural sugar.

Cooking methods

In lieu of using boiling water to cook fruits and vegetables, waterless methods are recommended as the pans made for this type of cooking do not reach boiling point inside; such pans are made of very heavy stainless steel with lids that fit securely, creating a vapour seal. Because of the low heat needed by this method of cooking, there is no escaping steam and therefore no odour, neither is there a chance for pressure to build up. These pans are more expensive than some other lighter types but are well worth the money. The advantage of stainless steel pans is that they may be used for frying, baking, or roasting on top of the stove, as they are completely 'non-stick' without being coated with a special substance.

Stir-frying

This is the fastest method of cooking which also retains the liquid, but the temperature of the food does reach a higher point. It is an excellent way of producing a meal quickly.

Steaming

Steaming is economical because the pans may be built up one upon another. The steamers I prefer are made of bamboo and are available from many Asian and Chinese shops. Buy one that fits your biggest pan, in this way you can steam dark green leaves in single layers, for about 1–2 minutes, just enough to turn the dark green into bright green. Provided you have removed the white vein from the centre of the leaves, have shredded them very finely and steamed them immediately, they will be slightly 'chewy' when served, have a delicious flavour and be full of nutrients.

All water from steaming or boiling of vegetables should be conserved, as it contains nutrients leached out during the cooking. Use this water for cooking grains, soups, or sauces.

Beans should be soaked for 8 hours before cooking. (The exception is the soya bean which needs soaking for 24 hours.) If left longer, change the soaking water. Before cooking, throw the soaking water away and bring the beans rapidly to the boil in fresh water. Continue boiling rapidly for 12 minutes then turn down to slow boiling. This will eliminate the harmful enzymes present in raw beans. When cooking beans, add a piece of dried seaweed, about 1 1/2 inches square - this has several advantages: the beans cook faster; flavour is improved; and the nutrients in the seaweed are leached out and absorbed by the beans. This method of cooking beans seems to assist in preventing gas forming in the stomach. Adding a 1/2-teaspoon of the herb savory, alone or in addition to seaweed, is also helpful. The cooking time of beans varies, not only with different types, but also with their age. Grains and lentils also benefit from pre-soaking, as this reduces the cooking time.

10. Acid-and alkaline-forming foods – getting the balance right

Blood carries oxygen to every cell in our bodies, together with nutrients which nourish and support all our internal systems. The blood then collects the waste material created by this process and returns it to the kidneys for evacuation, while carbon dioxide is returned to the lungs where it is exhaled. It is therefore of vital importance that we maintain our blood in a healthy condition, as any disturbance in the composition of body tissue will lead to poor health.

The blood plasma of a healthy person should be slightly alkaline. Acid/alkali balance is measured on a pH scale. Water, which is considered to be neutral, has a pH of 7. Any pH higher than this is alkaline, any pH lower is acid.

Acid- and alkali-*forming* foods should not be confused with acid foods and alkaline foods, which refers to their state before being consumed. Acid/alkali-*forming* foods are determined by the mineral residue within the body after the food is eaten, digested, absorbed and metabolized.

Acid-forming foods leave a residue of phosphorus, sulphur and chlorine, while *alkali*-forming foods leave a residue of sodium, potassium, calcium and magnesium. When all these chemical elements interact they produce body fluids of the correct pH balance.

The most acid-forming foods, therefore, which should be avoided or consumed only occasionally, are: meat, dairy produce and eggs. The extreme alkaline-forming foods are sugar, alcohol, and soft drinks with a high sugar content. Very acid-forming foods set up a craving for very alkaline-forming foods, and vice versa. Apart from these extremes most foods will be near the neutral range.

If approximately 60 per cent of the diet consists largely of vegetables (mostly leafy vegetables) and 20 per cent of fruit, there should be no problem of imbalance, as these are alkaline-forming, with the correct balance of sodium and potassium, and will leave 20 per cent of the diet for starch and protein. As most of us have existed on a predominantly acid diet all our lives, this should help considerably to correct the balance. It is this balance of foods, including 60 per cent from enzyme-rich raw sources, which helped me to control my arthritis.

Why we need enzyme-rich foods

Our bodies manufacture their own enzymes, but need support from those in the diet. Enzymes help the nutrients of the body to perform their tasks and are required for processes within the body where oxygen is used. They also help with digestion, growth, metabolism, and reproduction of cells. They act as catalysts within the cells to help other processes to continue.

11. Food combining

Of all foods there is one that must be eaten alone, as it does not mix happily with any other: melon. When it is eaten be sure not to eat anything else until 20 minutes have elapsed. It does not combine happily with other fruit. As all fruits pass through the stomach much faster than other foods, it is also advisable to wait 20 minutes after eating them before consuming other foods, as this will avoid digestive disturbances.

Concentrated proteins, i.e. meat, fish, and cheese, do not mix well with carbohydrates. (For this reason our dogs also benefit from two separate meals a day - one of meat, the other of biscuit, cereals and vegetable matter.) Some people are affected more than others, but most older people suffer from digestive disturbances caused by this. For further details on this subject consult *Food Combining for Health* by Doris Grant and Jean Joice.

12. Complex carbohydrates – why they are better than refined carbohydrates

Complex carbohydrates (otherwise known as polysaccharides) are obtained from whole foods; they are found in vegetables, fruits, beans, grains, nuts, seeds and sprouts. When these foods are eaten the fuel released by them flows at a slow, steady rate into the bloodstream, giving us a sustained energy level over several hours. Carbohydrates that have been refined, in contrast, convert very quickly into fuel, pour rapidly into the bloodstream and do not sustain energy levels.

Refined carbohydrates include white rice, white flour, and sugar. Foods made from them are lacking in fibre and few of the vitamins are returned during the enrichment process. Foods that provide only energy are 'empty' foods; because they do not contain the natural mix of nutrients, the body has to draw the balance from elsewhere, gradually depleting the store of nutrients in the body. Complex carbohydrates contain all the natural elements needed, and in the right proportion.

When more calories are consumed than are required by the body, from whatever source, they will be converted into fat and stored. A diet high in complex carbohydrates will be lower in fat, lower in calories, and higher in fibre. Fibre consists of digestible and indigestible elements, both of which are necessary for the efficient functioning of the bowel.

References

Your Personal Vitamin Profile, Dr Michael Colgan, Blond and Briggs, London.

The Good Nutrients Guide, Rita Greer and Dr Robert Woodward, Published by Rita Greer, 225 Putney Bridge Road, London SW15.

Food Combining for Health, Doris Grant and Jean Joice, Thorsons, London.

Of further interest. . .

Thorsons Complete Guide to Vitamins and Minerals

Leonard Mervyn B.Sc., Ph.D., C.Chem, F.R.S.C.

• The complete guide for both general and professional readers, compiled by a biochemist and leading authority on the subject, giving the latest information available on the full range of vitamins and minerals.

• As well as supplying general information on each of the vitamins and minerals, it includes details of supplementation regimes and the use of vitamins and minerals in conjunction with drugs prescribed by doctors.

The A-Z of Nutritional Health

Adrienne Mayes Ph.D

Never before has the connection between nutrition and health been
so widely recognised; daily we are bombarded with information on
the latest scientific findings, often in a confusing – sometimes contra-
dictory – fashion. *The A-Z of Nutritional Health* is an invaluable
handbook in helping to make sense both of the terminology of nutrition and the relation between nutrition and health.

- Highly accessible A-Z format allows quick access to information
- Covers all commonly used nutritional terms
- Clear, simple and scientifically accurate
- Illuminates connections between diet and health

Authoritative and up to date, *The A-Z of Nutritional Health* is
straightforward enough for the layperson and yet contains the detail
necessary for the health professional.